THE
YOUTH IN ACTION
BOOK

by
SHIRLEY POLLOCK

with illustrations by
VERONICA SCHARF

Meriwether Publishing Ltd., Publisher
P.O. Box 7710
Colorado Springs, CO 80933

Cover Design by Michelle Zapel
Edited by Arthur Zapel
Typography by Kathy Pijanowski

ISBN: 0-916260-29-1
Library of Congress Catalog Card Number: 84-061478
©Copyright MCMLXXXV Meriwether Publishing Ltd.
Printed in the United States of America
First Edition

To
Thomas and James Harmon,
the teen-agers in our family

INTRODUCTION

Youth and **action** go together like *astronaut* and *space shuttle*. Whether you are punching a computer or kicking a soccer ball, you are active and alive! It's all part of being a teen-ager.

Action: Hitting home runs. Breaking the relay tape at the finish line. Washing cars to add to church camp funds. Prancing through band formations. Singing in youth choirs. Even when you must be physically quiet, your mind races on, like the boy in study hall, bobbing his head in time to music, an invisible drum beating in his brain.

Youth and **action.** That's what this book is all about. Here are hundreds of activities to excite and challenge you. Many of them originated with teen-agers like yourself. They have been youth-tested and youth-tailored. For instance:

- Do you like to go places and explore new territory?

- Do you enjoy the company of your peers?

- Are you eager to learn new skills?

- Do you or your youth group need money?

- Are you tired of the same old parties?

- Do you enjoy doing some things by yourself?

- Are you into the arts? music? crafts?

- Do you like to pass on love and acceptance to those who suffer?

- Do you enjoy giving, as well as receiving?

- Do you ever take a hard look at yourself — and at what really counts in life?

If you answer *yes* to any of these questions, *The Youth in Action Book* is right for you. Flip through its pages. Find activities that appeal to you. Try them — and enjoy!

— Shirley Pollock

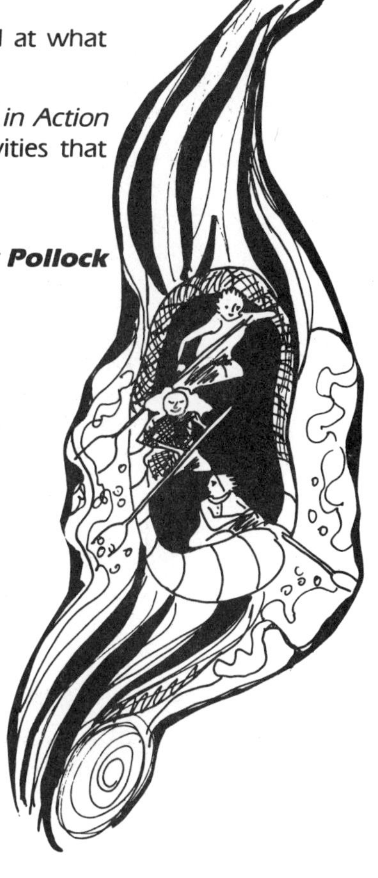

CONTENTS

CHAPTER 1:
CREATE! 1
Collage; Collect Shells for a Purpose; Create Your Own Cartoons; Create Your Own Puppets; Design House Floor Plans; Design Home Interiors; Develop and Enlarge Your Own Pictures; Garden on Your Window Ledge; Grow a Natural Garden; Invent Something; Learn a Dying Art or Skill; Make a Family Tree; Make and Furnish a Miniature Dollhouse; Make Old-Fashioned Toys; Make Potato Prints; Paint Abstracts; Paint Basement, Cellar or Stairwells; Sculpture in the Sand; Spin Yarn; Wallpaper; Write Poetry; More Creative Activities

CHAPTER 2:
GET TOGETHER WITH YOUR PEERS 31
Bicycle on a Tandem; Go Bowling; Breakfast in the Park; Converse with Friends and Strangers; Cross-Country Ski; Go Dutch Treat for Dining Out; Experiment with ESP (Extrasensory Perception); Fly a Kite; Hold a Box Social; Have a Bridal Gown Fashion Show; Have a Candy Pull; Have a Clown Party; Exchange White Elephants; Make Homemade Ice Cream; Have a Pancake Party; Hold a Progressive Board Game Party; Have a Roaring '20s Party; Have a Show-and-Tell Party; Go Skateboarding; Start a Rap Group; Tape-Record Your Friends; More Things to Do Together

CHAPTER 3:
GIVE YOURSELF AWAY 55
Band Birds; Be a Church Volunteer; Be a Community Services Volunteer; Be a Junior Firefighter; Be a Hospital Volunteer; Volunteer to Help the Mentally Handicapped; Help with Special Olympics for the Mentally Handicapped; Be Kind to Parents; Be Neighborly; Clean Up Local Parks and Streams; Collect Old Clothes for Charity Boxes; Crusade for a Cause; Dig up the Ground; Follow Your Good Intentions; Help with Meals on Wheels; Help with the World Hunger Problem; Organize a Summer Nursery School; Recycle Something; Shop at the Supermarket for Your Parents or Neighbors; Start a Baby-Sitting Class; Teach or Tutor; Teach Your Skill to Someone Else; Telephone a Loner; Visit the Elderly; Visit Veterans' Hospitals as Clowns

CHAPTER 4:
ENJOY SOLO ACTIVITIES 93
Brainstorm One-Time Things to Do; Change Your Physical Appearance; Check Up on Your Health Habits; Clean Your Room; Daydream and Make Your Dreams Come True; Transport Yourself to the Conductor's Stand; Express Yourself in Graffiti; Get Acquainted with Yourself; Keep a Happiness Book; Keep a Journal; Meditate; Start Running; Send for a Living Will; Shoo the Blues Away; Tape Yourself; Visit Your Grandmother; Write on an Impromptu Basis; Write Down Your Life Philosophy

CHAPTER 5:
GO WHERE THE ACTION IS 119
Attend Auctions; Attend Different Churches; Attend a Circus; Attend Folk Fairs; Attend a Garage Sale; Attend Hockey Games; Attend Motorcycle Races; Attend Old Car Exhibits; Attend a Seminar; Attend Symphony Concerts; Go Backpacking; Go Camping; Climb to the Top; Go Hang-Gliding;

Join a Bicycle Club; Mall-Hop to See Free Shows; Pick Fruits; Ride a Blimp; Ride to the End of the Line; Shoot the Rapids; Try Youth-Hosteling; Visit a Courtroom; Visit an Art Museum; Visit Historical Sites; Visit Libraries; Visit a Museum; Visit a Television Station; Visit a Theme Park; More Places to Go

CHAPTER 6:
STRETCH YOUR KNOW-HOW **153**
Act, Design Scenery and Create Lighting Effects; Be a Bibliomaniac; Be a Specialist; Brush Up on Etiquette; Collect Autographs; Collect Posters; Collect Words; Enroll in Summer Programs; Expand your Religious Knowledge; Get Acquainted with Ballet; Intern in a Profession, Trade or Business; Learn About Politics; Learn Handwriting Analysis; Learn Another Language; Learn a New Skill, Like Sign Language; Learn Scuba Diving; Learn Windsurfing; Listen; Organize a Writers' Club; Search for Scholarships and Loans; Study Palmistry; More Ways to Learn More

CHAPTER 7:
EARN DOLLARS AND SENSE **183**
Get a Job; Advertise Job Wanted, Service Offered or Item for Sale; Baby-Sit for Dollars; Create Your Own Business or Service; Buy and Sell Flowers Door-to-Door; Clean Carpets; Make Corsages; Make and Rent Costumes; Operate an Antique Photo Studio; Organize a Teen-age Job Agency; Refinish Furniture; Sell Balloons; Start a Second-Time-Around Business; Enter Contests; Get a Paper Route; Hold a Silent Auction; House-Sit; Join a Culinary Crew; More Money-Making Ideas

Create!

COLLAGE

"Organized Chaos," the cutline called the Mount Lebanon boy's room, pictured in the *Pittsburgh Press*. Walls, ceiling and floor screamed color and action. According to the featured story, this teen-ager had collaged every inch of his room, then varnished it with a permanent finish.

This is but one example of the hundreds of collage projects teenagers have created. So why not join the enthusiasts — if you haven't already?

1. **What is a collage?**
    According to the dictionary definition, it is "a kind of surrealist art in which bits of flat objects, as newspaper, cloth, pressed flowers, etc., are pasted together in incongruous relationship for their symbolic or suggestive effect."

    Teen-agers use many items to construct theirs: cut-out pictures and words from magazines; travel folders; greeting cards; snapshots of friends and family photos; picture postcards; church bulletins, playbills, sports programs; award ribbons, buttons, seals; anything that will stick — even three-dimensional items such as feathers, paper money, plastic toys and records.

    Backgrounds can be permanent or temporary. If you have a wall that needs painting or papering, glue objects directly to the wall surface. Otherwise, use banquet table paper, mill ends of newsprint rolls or simply old newspapers. Tape or tack these to walls you do not wish to permanently cover.

    The process of collaging is simple. Completely cover the background by superimposing paraphernalia that will stick and is not too heavy. Overlap items so that none of the background shows.

2. **What you collage, where, and why will depend on your own interests,** of course. However, to spark your creativity, here are more examples of what other teen-agers have fashioned:

4

- A sophomore blocked off sections of the basement family room walls for each member of the family to decorate. Everyone, from toddler to grandma, worked on the project for months. In the process, though, it became the talk of the neighborhood.

- Another teen-ager collaged one wall of his room with rock and roll celebrity photographs, programs of concerts he had attended, advertisements, handbills and album covers.

- A would-be traveler has his bedroom wall covered with maps, travel posters and folders, mounted on burlap that hangs from a pole, much like a picture frame.

- A novice writer covered a walk-in closet with rejection slips in a fascinating design. "If you look closely," he suggests, "you will find copies of my first checks for sales. I didn't want to make the picture too depressing."

- A youth who summers at Martha's Vineyard mounted driftwood, shells, bits of sponge, fishnet, seaweed and gulls' feathers (all beachcombings after a northeaster) into a porch wall collage.

- Above his desk, a novice photographer has grouped his picture-taking trials and errors.

- Another boy has collected family poses. Included are tin-types, daguerreotypes of ancestors who have lost their identity because someone failed to label the pictures. The collager has mounted his collection on three-ply veneer in a family tree design, minus studied chronological groupings.

- Using wallpaper samples from a discarded display book, another collage enthusiast created a "mod" design for her bed's headboard.

- Ann made a collage for her boyfriend — all about their dates together. She included anything related to their common interests. It was a picture diary.

Now it's your turn to collage. What will it be? Whatever — you will produce a self-portrait of sorts.

COLLECT SHELLS FOR A PURPOSE

Whatever happened to all those shells you collected as a youngster? For years they remained treasures, tucked away in drawers and cupboards. But where are they now?

"If you collect shells for a special reason, you will add value to your original discovery," says Christopher, a teen-aged conchologist. Following through on his suggestion, here are some shell-related activities:

1. **Use shells to decorate.**
    You can frame old mirrors, fill glass lamp bases, cover tabletops, appliqué lampshades and candy dishes or string small shells like bead ropes, to screen a doorway.

2. **Make jewelry** for yourself and for gifts. Loop strings of shells around your neck, dangle them from your ears or set them in brooch clasps.

    This art form is easy and cheap. Clean the shells thoroughly. When completely dry, cover with natural-colored nail polish. Buy hardware at any shell shop (where you can also get fuller instructions).

3. **Make pictures and novelty wall motifs.**
    Examples line restaurant and motel walls along the seacoasts. For these, you also need bits of sea oats, sea grape and driftwood.

4. **Find out about the strange habits of the creatures who live in those shells.** Such discoveries can be as hair-raising as a whodunit. Some of those creatures are killers (see Audrey Newell's book, *Sea Shells in Action*). These little creatures even eat each other up, cannibal-like.

    Take the whelk, for instance. It usually eats clams. When no clams are around, it eats other whelks. And worse yet, whelks eat each other inside the egg case.

It's a wait-and-move-fast technique under water. Crown conches wait until oysters open their shells. Then, presto! They devour the oyster before the shell clamps shut again.

Likewise, the harp waits for crabs. Only it allows the crab to eat its arrow-like foot. (It doesn't mind. It can grow another foot.) But while the crab is eating the harp's foot, the harp throws poison on the crab, dusts it in the sand and eats it for dinner.

Read about the dangers that lurk in the sea for the inhabitants of the shells you are collecting. Then you will see them with knowing eyes.

CREATE YOUR OWN CARTOONS

Sure, you read the newspaper comics, and comic books are old friends. But have you ever created your own cartoon characters?

Steve has. His characters are wild, flighty and rocket-propelled. He says there's no limit to what he can do with his super-heroes. Here is how he does it — and suggests you do it, too:

1. **Try to imagine characters as good and bad.**
    Use clever names and catchy costumes, though even a stupid character is feasible.

2. **Take an ordinary, everyday object and make it into something more.** For instance, a T-square becomes a multi-purpose sword. Paper clips are missiles. Leave the interpretation of the objects to the viewer.

3. **To further stimulate your own imagination for drawing comics, study your favorite comic strips.** Note the simple lines. Try copying a figure or two. Then let your own imagination guide your pencil, like a planchette over a ouija board. No one need see the results. And it's great self-entertainment.

CREATE YOUR OWN PUPPETS

In kindergarten, did you make peanut shell faces to put on your fingers? They helped you learn numbers. Remember? Or did you outline faces with magic marker on flat, round suckers? You poked the stick through a paper napkin that hung down over your wrist. And presto! You had a puppet that danced and recited nonsense rhymes.

That was kid stuff, of course. But adults enjoy puppets, too, and have through the centuries. For instance, did you know that Goethe wrote plays for the puppet theater in the 18th century? Mozart and Haydn wrote music for it. And today in Salzburg, Austria, a marionette theater presents grand opera. So you see, you are carrying on a sophisticated art tradition when you make your own puppets.

1. **Start with hand puppets,** since they are the easiest to make and use. They move as readily as your hand. You can make them from scraps.

2. **You may choose from many kinds of hand puppets. Cloth and head puppets** vary according to their heads. Make them from plasticene (or any other type of oily clay) or papier maché, forming them around your index finger.

   Use potatoes or apples. (Dried apples are favorites in Appalachian crafts.) Cut a hole in the bottom big enough for your finger. Or use rubber, tennis, ping-pong or styrofoam balls for heads.

   Paint on facial features, or for potato and apple heads, use thumbtacks and pinned-on beads to outline mouths, noses and eyes. Glue on yarn or frayed twine for hair. Insert your index finger into the head, and wrap your fist in a cloth (handkerchief, scarf or napkin).

   Cloth cut-out puppets can hold things in their hands. Cut a paper doll figure, 12" high, out of sturdy fabric (with material folded so you have two identical figures). Stitch the two pieces (front and back) together and turn inside-out.

From pieces of felt, make hands and sew onto arms. Use cotton, yarn or an old doll's wig for hair. Stuff head with shredded old nylons. Stitch across the neck, allowing only enough room for your finger to project into the head. Facial features may be either painted or appliquéd on. In the place of the cloth head, you have a choice of any of the other heads mentioned above, but secure your choice permanently to the cloth body.

To manipulate the cloth cut-out puppet, put your thumb in one arm, index finger in the head and middle finger in the other arm.

Knitted puppets made their debut in card shops during a holiday season. If you knit, you will enjoy working with these for animal characters.

Get Disneyland characters for patterns. Use brightly-colored scraps of yarn — several different colors for various parts of the puppet. Knit like a mitten that comes over your wrist. Instead of the thumb being at right or left, knit a wide, wide thumb across the front, to be used as the lower jaw of the mouse or dog.

Glue on bits of colored felt for nose, eyes and tongue. Sew on scraps of yarn for hair and whiskers. Manipulate with four fingers in the mitten top and thumb in the area knitted for the lower jaw.

3.   **Once you have created your own puppets, you have many more creative activities awaiting you.** Progress to making jointed marionettes (operated by strings). Build a puppet stage. Write plays or musicals for puppet shows. Adapt stories to act out, from *Winnie the Pooh* to "David and Goliath." Teach children how to make puppets. Put on puppet shows for children's hospitals, nursing homes, senior citizens' centers and churches.

DESIGN HOUSE FLOOR PLANS

Have you ever tried drawing house plans? Without benefit of mechanical drawing and architectural design, your ideas may go wild. But who cares? Your dream house is on paper, at least. And more than one young couple has adapted way-out plans to fit their first custom-built home.

1. **Your designs can turn into livable plans,** too, with a little guidance. Scan newspaper real estate sections, or free real estate advertising booklets (found by supermarket entrances).

    Check features that denote good living: lots of closet space, built-in cupboards and shelves, adequate window exposure for light or energy conservation, roomy entrances and convenience of bathroom to bedrooms and of kitchen to dining area. Clip out plans that appeal to you.

    Adapt your already-created plans to a kitchen from one, a bedroom from another, a family room from a third. Potpourri? Perhaps. But you can learn a lot from such adaptations if you follow through with the exact scale used.

2. **Your next possible step is to visit model homes and condominiums in real estate developments.** There you will receive advertising brochures with detailed to-scale plans of the models.

    Lots of people "just look." So you will be no exception. Besides, young people *are* prospective buyers — if not now, then later. Thus, you can be sure of courteous treatment by the salespeople. Ask intelligent questions based on your cut-out plan experience, exude enthusiam, and you will be welcome, never fear.

    You can travel from open house to open house if you check newspaper listings. Compare the plans. Look beyond the decorating and surface features. Note the easy flow or awkwardness of passage from one room to another. Look for openness and convenience of room arrangement. Think of yourself as living there. What features please? What couldn't you live with? Note whether there is a focal point. Is there a fireplace or other special area that would be the gathering place for family and friends?

3. **Viewing models while carrying the floor plan** will help you later view your own designs in three dimensions. Open spaces in the wall lines that represent doors and windows take shape. You see walls as lengths of space for pictures and furniture. Room heights become important dimensions.

    Now you can go back to the first brainstormed plans and put together a realistic house floor design. And perhaps someday you may use it. A dream home *can* become real.

DESIGN HOME INTERIORS

Hopping from open house to model home, studying floor plans, opens up another activity — interior decorating. You may enjoy pursuing any one or all of the following categories: furniture, carpeting, draperies or interior accessories.

1. **Using the same follow-through you did with house plans, cut out pictures of decorated rooms from magazines.** Note color combinations, textures of wood and fabric and style of furniture. Also, check combinations of style and finish of furnishings within a single room.

2. **If this initiation to interior decoration fascinates you, browse through your library's art department for books on interior design.** Shuffle through the pages, pausing at pictures.

    Note designers' technical terms used in describing the interior scene. You may want to jot down some of the vocabulary, such as: "life-style furnishings," "Art Deco-style desk," graphics from a series of "visuals," "machine-aesthetic stereo components" and "shell chair." Future visits to furniture stores, lighting fixture shops and decorating studios will be more meaningful once you have armed yourself with a few choice terms.

3.   Now invade a furniture store.
When asked, "May I help you?" give the accepted answer: "Thank you. I'm just looking." The salesperson will then say, "If I can be of service, please let me know. Here is my card."

In most furniture stores, you have freedom to roam as long as you wish. An intelligent question, from time to time, will add to your knowledge.

You may find your furniture-browsing more exciting if you concentrate on one thing, such as high-rise beds or glass-topped fruitwood coffee tables. While giving you a reason for looking, the search becomes a game, like a scavenger hunt.

A further reason for your pursuit can be decorating your own room. Whether or not you actually do redecorate, plan all the possibilities. Seek out the exact pieces you would use, were you making those changes. This costs you nothing, and gives purpose to your window-shopping. And it will make you knowledgeable about decorating, way beyond: "I'll die if I can't have that glass-topped chrome desk!"

DEVELOP AND ENLARGE YOUR OWN PICTURES

Instead of dropping your finished rolls of film at the Kodak hut or supermarket for processing, make yourself a darkroom. Then watch the magic of chemistry transform your film. By slipping a piece of paper into a tray of chemical, you will see an image develop on the paper.

1. **This film process involves three steps:** developing the film, which gives you the negatives from which you make the prints; making contact prints of the negative, so you can see what the picture will look like; and making an enlargement.

2. **How do you learn this activity?**
    Apprentice under a professional or super amateur photographer. Get private instruction. Or enroll in a class sponsored by the city recreational department, a church or scout groups.

    You can teach yourself, of course. All sorts of guides are on sale at camera shops. Magazines about photography are on all newsstands.

    A recommended book for beginners is *The Basic Darkroom Book*, by Tom Grimm (a Plume book, New American Library, Inc.). Step by step, it tells how to develop black and white and color prints. It also teaches tricks, such as how to save underexposed film by "pushing" the development.

GARDEN ON YOUR WINDOW LEDGE

Big as a barrel or small as a hat — any container that holds soil can become a small garden on your window ledge, terrace or rooftop.

1. **Raise zinnias and marigolds in an old cowboy boot** (lacquered inside and out to keep the leather from rotting). Raise tomatoes, lettuce, peppers or zucchini in flowerpots placed outside your window, on ledge or roof. Grow strawberries in safety hats (with a hole bored in the bottom of each), perched on sewer pipe. All you need is a bit of ingenuity, garden soil and compost, with a little fertilizer occasionally thrown in for good measure.

2. **Full information for growing gardens in containers** is printed in a United States Printing Office booklet — "Growing Vegetable Gardens in Containers." Write to Consumer Information Center, 669F, Pueblo, CO 81009.

Some of the facts included in this material are as follows: you must have at least five hours of full sun. The container should be large enough to accommodate roots and plants, and have space enough to allow good air circulation and frequent watering. The booklet even suggests that corn can be raised in a container if the holder is large enough. Can't you see a corn stalk on your window ledge, teasing the neighbors?

GROW A NATURAL GARDEN

A garden you don't have to weed? It sounds impossible. But with a natural garden — encouraged by the environmental awareness movement across the United States — weeds make up the garden. You work for the natural look.

1. **Wildflowers that would be considered weeds in a conventional garden, you allow to bloom to attract butterflies.** When the blossoms go to seed, birds feed on them. You don't cut the grass within the garden, either. Supposedly, it only reaches 18 inches and then bends over. Bring in wildflowers that you have rescued from construction sites, where bulldozers would otherwise destroy them.

2. **However, you may have to educate your family and neighbors to the natural plan.** Point out these facts to them: You won't have to spend money on commercial fertilizers, insecticides or weed-killers. And crab grass does not grow when you don't mow.

   If they still think your natural garden is too shaggy for their manicured neighborhood, compromise. Add a split-rail fence to hide nature's abundant growth. Or hedge with cedar seedlings you've salvaged from road construction areas (if you have been lucky enough to find them).

INVENT SOMETHING

You are never too young to invent something, at least for your own use. And once your brain sparks to inventive ideas, who knows where your creations will lead you?

Take the experiences of Gene Deans, for instance. When he was 6 years old, he had the fastest bike on the block because he concocted a way to fasten a flywheel to the front tire. Since then, he has made many things, some of which are on the market: retractable soap on a rope (worn in the shower), a digital toy, an automobile floor mat that never shows dirt and Seal-a-Bag. (His dislike for soggy potato chips packaged in unsealed bags led to this last invention.)

Such an ordinary thing as a knot has to be thought up by somebody. A British doctor, Edward Hunter, invented the first new knot in 20 years. He used it for suturing, since it works well with nylon string. Now the Hunter knot takes its place along with the double-reef (used to tie shoestrings) and the clove-hitch (used on neckties).

1. **Sometimes inventive ideas come to you in a sudden flash, instead of your having experimented over and over again —** something you don't invent, exactly. But you discover a new use for what already exists.

   That's how the Slinky toy originated. Richard James worked for the Cramp Shipyard in Philadelphia, trying to eliminate vibrations in the delicate instruments of a vessel. One of the coil springs he was using fell from a shelf, walked across a pile of books and bounced to the floor.

   "It's a toy," thought James. And at that moment, Slinky was born. Today, Slinky is still walking down stairs in homes all over the world, just as it has in your house, no doubt.

2. **Inventing, then, comes about in two ways.**
   Grab that lightning flash as it strikes, and you may end up with a $4 million business, as James has. Or use time, determination and effort, as Thomas Edison did. His was a lifetime of

experimenting, with only catnaps between tries. Yet he is still serving you daily with his breakthroughs in lighting, movies, phonographs, cameras and synthetic rubber, to name a few.

Humanitarian or millionaire — or both. Take your choice. Try inventing something, though, in your spare time.

LEARN A DYING ART OR SKILL

Some exciting crafts depend on teen-agers to restore them to their former level of wonder and beauty. Some examples: hand-carving furniture, glass-blowing, quilting, reupholstering, staining glass.

1. **Let's take invisible china-repairing for a special example,** because it takes steady hands and keen eyesight. And young people are the best-qualified that way. This is a craft that only 30 or so people in the United States have master-ed. The art is to repair museum pieces, heirlooms and ordinary porcelain to look like the rest of the object. Even a figurine broken into 75 pieces can be repaired by these craft-artists. For museum objects, both painting and sculpturing go into constructing missing parts to match the object.

2. **For further enlightenment about this craft, read *Repairing and Restoring Glass,*** by William Karl Klein. Can you imagine yourself repairing a 12th century Sung bowl, Ming vases or Meissen porcelain figurines? Why not learn to put together your grandmother's bone china teacup without a trace of breakage showing? What an art!

MAKE A FAMILY TREE

If the genealogy bug bites you, you'll scratch for facts in all sorts of strange places, like Don. He's traveling to a governor's mansion, where part of his family tree is recorded on an entrance wall. Your search may take you to New Zealand or Finland. who knows, unless you start scratching?

1. **Start with yourself in your search for family tree information.** Jot down statistics you know about your siblings, parents, grandparents and yourself, of course. Then work backward, filling in the unknowns as you talk to other relatives.

2. **Pick your parents' memories next.**
Ask to see any records, clippings, papers and memorabilia they have kept through the years. Quiz them for details on relationships and family history as they remember it being told to them.

3. **Also, ask questions of aunts and uncles.**
They will remember stories they have heard which your parents may not recall. Have them identify pictures left blank so far and events and family relationships thus far unexplained.

4. **Grandparents and great-grandparents are your best sources for reaching back.** They are your closest links with ancestors and can reveal exciting, surprising facts. Sue, for example, discovered an early Ingham County (Michigan) history book in her grandparents' library. In it was a complete account of her grandmother's mother's family from the time they migrated from the state of New York.

5. **Family reunions are excellent settings for finding out who knows what.** Older members will be pleased to tell their stories to teen-agers. They will also feed each other's memories, with the oldest recalling early events very clearly. Take notes, though, or you won't remember half of what you hear. Ask about records, clippings and papers that you may borrow to copy and then return.

For instance, at one such reunion, Janellen learned that her great-aunt had framed and hung on her bedroom wall the marriage license of Janellen's great-great-grandparents. This certificate confirmed proper spelling of names that Janellen needed.

While at reunions (or elsewhere), inquire about old family Bibles — the giant-sized, leather-bound editions that rested on marble-topped tables in the parlors of bygone days. Between the Old and New Testaments were often pages for marriage, birth and death records. You will have fairly accurate family statistics in any such books you uncover.

6. **Another personal source for family history is the town old-timer —** that person who takes it upon himself to keep track of everybody and their ancestors. Every town has one.

7. **Your county courthouse is your next best resource — provided your forebears lived in your county.** Otherwise, you have to travel to another county.

The county recorder's office provides the following information: deeds, mortgages, discharges from military service, plotting of cities and towns, adoptions, divorces and wills.

In addition, the county clerk's office keeps records concerning: probate and civic court orders, marriage applications and licenses, wills and receipts from estate settlements. Here, you can sleuth for hours.

8. **Also, county libraries are treasure houses** of county origins, atlases and histories of early inhabitants. You will find their files of old newspapers useful, too, for death notices and obituaries (once you have approximate dates with which to work).

9. **Likewise, your state library has resources you may want,** such as early settlement histories; census figures; and volumes of grave listings and grave marker photographs, prepared by Revolutionary and Civil War patriotic organizations.

10. **You will also want to explore old cemeteries,** once you know where your ancestors are buried. Take several pieces of chalk with you. Whiten the weathered gravestone letters to help you decipher dates and names.

11. **Telephone books are additional sources for family history.** In cities where members of your family have lived, look up the family name. Contact anyone who seems like a possible relative — shirttail or otherwise. Also, get in touch with historical and genealogical societies listed in those telephone books. They might have family leads.

12. **And lastly — or perhaps you should put this first — get your hands on a simple, clear instruction book on tracing ancestors.** Book stores and libraries offer many such volumes. A good one for beginners is *Genealogy*, by Kenn Stryker-Rodda (Brunswick, New Jersey, Boy Scouts of America — a merit badge pamphlet).

MAKE AND FURNISH
A MINIATURE DOLLHOUSE

Making and furnishing dollhouse miniatures are the fastest-growing hobbies in America, according to industry sources. And along with adults, young people are getting into these because they like to create their own color schemes and make their own furniture.

- Sonya, for example, raves about her dollhouse. "I do all my own wallpapering and painting," she explained. "I've made quilted bedspreads, needlepointed chair seats and braided rugs for it.

  "My friend, Anna, has a more elaborate dollhouse. Very expen-·sive. Only her dad does all the work. She can't select her own colors or styles of furniture. It's an elegant display, though. Her family has it in their living room, for everyone to admire. But I'd rather have my own creation," Sonya concluded.

- Ed makes no apology for helping his sister with her dollhouse. "There's a certain magic in working with wood, in shaping tiny pieces of furniture. I think I like the artistic challenge — or maybe I'm proud of my manual dexterity."

- Brenda has her boyfriend helping her restore a Victorian dollhouse that once belonged to her grandmother. "It has 10 rooms and a cupola, all badly in need of repair. "But we'll have an antique worth hundreds of dollars when we finish," she said.

Are you interested? Then here's how to get started.

1. **Begin with a shadow box, if you want to keep down expenses.**
Use various-sized shoe boxes, glued together. One teen-ager adapted hot lead type trays, discarded when computerized typesetting took over the newspaper business. She found them in a junkyard. On the market are corrugated shadow boxes you can stack or connect for houses. Occasionally, you can find precut cardboard dollhouses you punch out and glue.

2. **Borrow do-it-yourself books from the library.**
You will find that scale-model dollhouses, like the ones found in these four books, will be of considerable help: *A Family Dollhouse*, by Sara B. Stein (Viking); *The Most Wonderful Dollhouse Book*, by Millie Hines (Butterick); *Shaker Miniature Furniture*, by Cynthia and Jerome Rubin (VanNostrand Reinhold); and *Make Your Own Miniature Rooms*, by Estelle Ansley Worrell (Hobby House Press, distributed by Scribner's).

3. **As your project grows, you may want to invest** in your own how-to books, needlework kits for rugs, furniture, upholstery and other accessories, which are for sale along with room furniture. Buy only what you cannot make for yourself, however, if you wish to be creative. Watch costs, or you can spend too much for what can be a simple hobby.

MAKE OLD-FASHIONED TOYS

With no fuel and no batteries, your great- and great-great-grandparents played with toys powered by heat, sun and gravity — or by hand. And now you can re-create some of these 19th century playthings as easily as you can make paper airplanes — well, almost.

Simply follow the easy step-by-step directions and diagrams found in *Naturally Powered Old-Time Toys* (a book by Marjorie Henderson and Elizabeth Wilkinson, J.B. Lippincott Company). It includes patterns for 30 moving Victorian age toys. You can make a model of the first steam engine on record; you can construct a floating ferris wheel, a galloping horse and rider, a sun yacht, airplanes that carry messages, a monkey on a string, a bow-top kite, sunshine engines and dancing dolls.

Tools for making these playthings are inexpensive, usually. The most involved is a soldering iron. Materials are common household bits and pieces, such as wood, cardboard, paper, tin, wire — mostly discards. Time needed for making these toys varies from one to five hours.

MAKE POTATO PRINTS

You're kidding!" exclaimed Jody, as she fingered the block-print draperies in Ellen's bedroom. "These are potato prints? You're crazy! Where did you get them? I want a pair for my room."

"I made them, and you can, too," Ellen said.

"But how?"

"With potatoes. Ever since I read in a hobby book about an exclusive designer in New York who was asking $300 for a pair of hand-woven potato-printed draperies, I figured potato-printing was my dish. It's the simplest type of relief printing. And cheap. Make a mistake in cutting the design. Throw the offending potato away and reach for another."

Indeed, Ellen's potato prints are as attractive as many others made with more sophisticated techniques. If you would like to try potato-printing a border on a skirt or a design on a T-shirt, here are basic procedures to follow:

1. **Select a large, firm potato.**

2. **Sketch a simple design to fit the potato's size.** Use tracing paper and blacken the back side with a soft lead pencil. Remember that the design will be in reverse when printed.

3. **Cut the potato either lengthwise or crosswise.**

4. **Transfer your design to the cut-open surface of the potato.** Place the tracing paper on the printing surface. Re-trace the design.

5. **Cut away the sections of the potato not needed for the raised design.** Gouge with a sharp paring knife. Cut about ⅛" deep. Only the design will remain raised.

6. **With a small brush, apply special ink for fabrics to the raised surface.** Check with an art supply store for washable paint or ink.

7. **Press evenly against the material.** Have material on a flat, hard surface. Keep the material free of wrinkles.

8. **Re-ink the potato design each time you print.**

    If you like potato-printing, you may want to also try linoleum printing, woodcuts, etching, engraving and drypoint.

PAINT ABSTRACTS

Did you see the cartoon that showed two boys standing on their heads, looking at an abstract painting? The caption read: "It's upside-down this way, too." At a high school art department public exhibit, two students met a similar reaction to their paintings.

- In defending his, Norman said, "What I paint as abstract is not supposed to be understood by anyone except *me*. It is an art form that only one person understands, but other people may enjoy. The only one who understands it is the artist."

- Ellen explained her abstract art in detail. "Abstract painting is a combination of shapes and forms put together without any particular design. It gives variety. It brings out texture and unusual patterns. Abstract art shows the individual's interpretation of an idea, either physically or psychologically observed. It deals with the mind more than the eyes."

If these quotes don't define abstract art clearly, take *Webster's* explanation for abstract in art: ". . . characterized by design or form that is geometric or otherwise not representational."

1. **Now that you have some concept of what abstract art is all about, try it yourself.** Express your ideas in shapes and colors without concern for realism. Don't worry that your brother will say it's freakish.

    Create your own "Dog Barking at the Moon." You will see the dog. Your friends probably won't, but who cares? You can express a lot of hang-ups and hopes in abstract art.

2. **A reverse of abstract painting is fun, too.** Study carefully a Picasso or Jackson Pollock painting. Convert it into a realistic picture, as you interpret it. This may take more talent, however. Realism isn't all that simple — except with a camera.

PAINT BASEMENT, CELLAR OR ATTIC STAIRWELLS

"You can have the wilds of Africa in your own home with just the swish of a paintbrush," says Anna May. At least that's all *she* did to transform her family's basement stairwell into a tropical jungle.

Anna May is clever with a brush. Realistic, too. Tigers lurk behind trees. Elephants trumpet their way through the brush. Exotic vegetation and multi-colored birds give life and excitement to a once-upon-a-time ugly, drab entrance.

1. **Almost every home has an uninspired area you can paint.** Probably yours is no exception. Tri-level homes are the modern version of the stairwell syndrome. Older houses have high-ceilinged wells to basement or attic.

2. **Whether or not you are experienced with the paintbrush, go creative!** Brighten the dark corners with flashing colors. Be bold! Be daring! Be original!

   - Bonnie was. In fact, she did her walls so abstractly that she has to interpret the murals to everyone who views them. "Except children," she explains. "They see elephants and giraffes I didn't even know were there. Four-year-old Teddy can see a camel with a baseball, and a cow wearing a beret with a feather!"

   - A boy in Milwaukee painted a realistic woods and water scene in his family's cellar stairwell. It was two stories high and he worked from a ladder. The novelty of his mural was the symbolism. Each item painted represented a friend or neighbor.

   For example, the owl in a tree was the optometrist who lived next door. The beaver gnawing at a log was his grandfather, who had just received the Beaver award for outstanding service to the Boy Scouts. A patch of purple flowers represented his girlfriend. (Yes, her name was Violet). True, the likenesses were difficult to figure out. But everyone viewing the mural enjoyed the guessing game — and wanted to be included. Thus, the panorama became a continued story.

SCULPTURE IN THE SAND

Two small children ran up and down the beach, begging lazy sun bathers to come and see. "It's a flying horse! A beautiful flying horse!"

Sure enough, someone with real talent had left a bas relief sculpture for the tide to wash away in a couple of hours. For the artist, the fun had been in the creating.

1. **You, too, can create sand pictures in bas relief.** Try sculpturing in your brother's sandbox or at the beach. All you need is sand, water and lots of patience to bring to life your own prancing horse.

2. **Or you can kibitz** while professional sand sculptors form pictures in three dimensions. If you are lucky enough to be in Ocean City, New Jersey, at the right time, you can watch contestants prepare their sand art for the annual contests. One is in July and one in August. Everything from American flags to a replica of da Vinci's *Last Supper* takes form as artists work and people watch.

The St. Petersburg, Florida, City Recreational Department holds a sand-sculpturing contest for children and young adults at the end of their summer program. Check your area. If there is sand and water, someone is sure to be sculpting.

SPIN YARN

Spinning yarn, a necessity of bygone days, today is a hobby for doctors, engineers and teen-agers. Therefore, you, too, may find it fascinating — if you have the time.

1. **Go to any historic house that is open to the public,** and chances are good that you will find an attendant in Early American costume, spinning away.

   At Pittsburgh, Pensylvania's South Park, a woman spins daily in a house on the Whiskey Rebellion site. In Gatlinburg, Tennessee, spinning demonstrations go on inside and outside the gift shops. And at the Medieval Festival sponsored by New College and Ringling Museum in Sarasota, Florida, demonstrations start with the shearing of sheep and continue through the weaving of cloth. Chat with these demonstrators, wherever you find them. Ask questions, and you will get answers that will help you teach yourself.

2. **Next, find yourself a spinning wheel.** If possible, find one you can try on before you buy. Then you will know how serious you are about spinning your own yarn for sweaters. Some community centers, YMCAs and YWCAs, churches and school domestic science departments own them for class use. If you buy, you can choose from several makes: Canadian, Castle and Charney.

3. **Once you have a good wheel, you need the right fleece.** Many weavers use wool from Lincolnshire, Cheviet or Marino sheep. Their wool is softer. Fibers twist easier.

4. **Next, you prepare the wool.** First, pick out foreign substances, such as dirt, sticks and burrs. Carding follows. Comb to disentangle the wool. This is done between two comb-like tools called "cards."

After carding, you have two choices: wash the wool and add oil to it before you start spinning; or you can spin unwashed wool, thus using the natural lanolin to keep the fibers together.

5. **The actual spinning takes much practice.**
You have to learn to avoid knots and bulges in the yarn. In time, though, you will get a feel for good yarn and know when you have a smooth treadle, which makes soft, even yarn.

6. **Once you have spun the yarn, you dye it.**
Try natural dyes. Goldenrod makes a bright yellow; marigolds, a greenish-yellow; ferns, green; poke berries, red.

Spinning is a craft worth trying. For once you have a wheel and cards, you can make three sweaters out of the yarn you spin from one fleece.

WALLPAPER

Clumsy comedians glue their hands in their pockets and wrap themselves in wallpaper until they look like mummies. But that doesn't mean you will — if you follow simple directions.

1. **You don't need to be professional to paper your own room or closet.** True, professional paper-hanging requires a working knowledge of mathematics, color and chemistry. As an amateur, though, you can get by with good manual dexterity — enough to hang the paper straight, match up designs and angle with crooked walls, if you have any.

2. **To avoid that "never again!" beginner's response, practice first.** Use cardboard cut-outs to get experience in papering corners, around doors and window sills. Or paper a doll's house.

3. **More expensive pre-pasted papers are the easiest to handle, experienced amateurs say.** Begin with straight, smooth surfaces. Follow directions that come with the rolls.

4. **Make your first project a simple one.**
Ruth A. papered one wall of her bedroom after practicing on her dollhouse. Todd bought a three-paneled scene of a Madrid bullfight. "I read the directions carefully," he says, "dipped the sheets in the bathtub, one at a time, and managed to match up the picture parts quite smoothly."

WRITE POETRY

By the time you are 20, you will have written a poem — to your car, your dog, your girlfriend or boyfriend. Don't laugh. Such verses are famous. For instance, Robert Burns wrote "An Ode to a Louse," which is still printed in English literature books.

1. **A fun way to start writing poetry is to use patterns you already know.**

Take the lyrics on the dust cover of your favorite record, for example. You know the beat as well as your own name. Only this time, mark it. Use an accent sign (´) on a syllable where the beat is stressed. For an unstressed syllable, use a short symbol (˘). Or practice with a nursery rhyme:

Twínklĕ, twínklĕ, líttlĕ stár.

Now make up your own words to fit the beat of your particular song. For instance:

Frećklĕs, frećklĕs ońh mў noŝe.

2. **The haiku is a precisely patterned poetic form** that teen-agers enjoy composing. The classic haiku is so clearly defined in mood and structure that it deserves more than cursory study. Save that until later.

For now, concern yourself with the single picture thought that is the basis of the haiku. The accepted English pattern has five syllables in lines one and three, and seven syllables in line two. Rhyming is not necessary. An example:

> While we are apart
> On different continents,
> We see the same moon.

3. **Still another fun form with a precise pattern is the cinquain —** so named because it has five lines. One favorite arrangement is as follows:

Line 1: state your theme in one word.

Line 2: use two words to describe the theme.

Line 3: in three words, give the action connected with the theme.

Line 4: use four words to denote a feeling connected with the theme.

Line 5: present a one-word synonym for the first word in the poem. To illustrate this arrangement:

> Tests.
> Cramming time.
> I am studying.
> I feel confident, ready.
> Examinations.

4. **You may enjoy writing nonsense verses,** such as those written by Ogden Nash and James Thurber.

5. **Or limericks may intrigue you —** that special variety of nonsense made popular by Edward Lear. The limerick has five anapestic lines — that is, each metrical foot has two short (˘) syllables, followed by one long (´) syllable.

The rhyme scheme is *a a b b a.* (That is, the first, second and last lines have three stresses; the third and fourth, two stresses.) For example:

> Săd-făced clówn walkĕd ăroúnd ŏn hĭs hańds
> Whĭle thĕ áudĭeńce cheéred ĭn thĕ stánds.
> Stĕp ăsíde, sŏmbĕr eýes,
> Whĭle yoŭr feét sĕe thĕ skíes,
> Thĕ trăpeźe ĭs thĕ wíre fŏr yoŭr hańds.

6. Of course, the easiest poetic form is free verse.
Its name gives it away. You have freedom.

You can use all kinds of rhythmic variations. Stanza divisions may be irregular and unusual. Rhyme is loose, or there is no rhyme. Punctuation, including capitalization, may be wanting, as with e e cumming's poetry. (His pen name mimicked his writing style.)

This may be your forte. If so, start with free verse after you have read many samples. Note, though, that it isn't prose. Free verse has rhythm. It has a subject — a theme. It is rich in figures of speech. It creates mood, feeling. It is poetry as practiced by Walt Whitman.

MORE CREATIVE ACTIVITIES:

Bake **bread.** Build a **raft.** Make your own **picture frames.** Make up a new **game.** Write a **short story, novel** or **play.** Make your own **furniture.** Build a **playhouse** for your kid brother. **Carve** wood or soap. Write **prayers** and **responsive readings.** Do a **silk screen. Quilt.** Tie **flies for fishing. Embroider, appliqué** or **paint pictures** on shirts and skirts. Make **Christmas cards** and **wrappings.** Sew **doll clothes.** Make **models** of boats, automobiles and planes. Build an **automobile** from junkyard parts. Make a **scrapbook** of recipes. Write a **song.** Create a **movie** (super-8 or 16 millimeter). Design your own **clothes.** Build a **miniature golf course** in your backyard. Create your own **gourmet recipes.** Write **letters to the editor** of your local newspaper.

Get Together With Your Peers

BICYCLE ON A TANDEM

Riding a bicycle built for two is a surprising venture, especially if you sit in the rear. Teamwork is the secret to successful tandem riding. The front pedaler steers, brakes and controls the gears. The back pedaler supplies muscle power and balance. Usually the girl rides in back, but not to play up the back-seat driver routine. Rather, the tandem works better if the lighter weight person rides in the rear.

Most bicycle rental agencies have at least one tandem bicycle. And if you are lucky, you may find a double tandem — a bike for four pedalers. This works the same as the tandem. The front rider still does all the steering, braking and gear-shifting. The three followers provide added leg work and balance. The four-person team has to synchronize the pedaling as smoothly as a rowing team must move in a single rhythm.

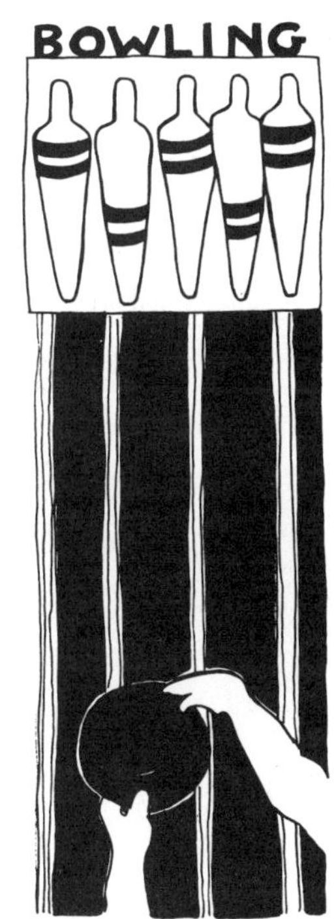

GO BOWLING

You don't have to bowl a perfect score (300) to have a good time. Even belonging to a league doesn't mean you roll strikes or spares every time. (You have a handicap.) Maybe that's why the game is so popular — you can take it or leave it, depending on how serious you are about the game.

If you have never played this ancient German indoor sport (introduced in America by the Dutch in the 17th century), here's what it's all about:

It is played on an alley, by rolling a ball at 10 maple pins. A regulation bowling alley is constructed of polished wood and measures 42 inches wide and 60 feet from foul line to center of the head pin. You throw a ball, which has two or three finger holes and weighs 10 to 16 pounds. The ball knocks down the pins, which are 15 inches high and set up in a triangular formation (in rows of one-four) at the opposite end of the alley.

A bowling game is divided into 10 frames, with two throws allowed you in each frame, if needed. Each toppled pin counts as one point. Knocking down all pins in the first throw is called a strike and scores 10 points, plus the total of the next two throws. Clearing the alley with two balls is a spare and scores 10 points plus the next throw. Thirteen consecutive strikes is a perfect game.

Modern bowling lanes are clean, cheerful, brightly lighted and electronically equipped. Because they are crowded with teams in season, your chances to roll a few games with a friend or two are limited. Grab those off hours: weekends — all day; evenings — 9:30-midnight, or all night in some lanes. A teens' all-night bowling party is one way to stay out late, if you stay put or have chaperons.

If possible, bowl the first few times with a friend who has had enough experience to give you the necessary pointers and to do the scoring. Once you know your game, join a league or start a team of your own. It's cheaper. You have something to do once a week at a designated time. You have competition based on ability, with prizes and banquets at the end of the season.

Check your own neighborhood for either open or league opportunities. It is not a cheap sport at best, but those who like it are dedicated to the exercise and social activity it offers.

BREAKFAST IN THE PARK

Have you ever slithered out of bed in the shadowy dawn to breakfast in the park? Any park will do, like the Garden of the Gods (a scenic rock formation park) in Colorado Springs, Colorado. The experience is worth a rerun — or initiation, if this idea is new to you.

You will want to be selective about whom you ask to join you. All teenagers aren't that ready to greet the dawn. But if you can find one or two buddies who enjoy sunrises and the great out-of-doors, share the high.

1. **Pack your picnic the night before.**
   Remember the frying pan and eggs. And don't forget bacon and charcoal, for the aroma of frying bacon, mixed with the scent of burning charcoal, becomes heady in the moist early morning air.

2. **Try to select a special cove, a mountaintop, a ledge overlooking the river** — whatever your particular park holds that is a picture postcard view.

3. **Turn up your hearing aid (a metaphor, of course) and tune in** on wren trills, the show-and-tell of a mocking bird dizzily dancing and singing for his mate. The sights and sounds are what make breakfast in the park a special event, no matter what food your tote bag contains. Companions who are sensitive to the shimmering magic will enhance your pleasure. Otherwise, a breakfast in the park can also be a satisfying solo flight.

CONVERSE WITH FRIENDS AND STRANGERS

"If you talk about yourself, you are a bore. If you talk about others, you are a gossip. If you talk about *me*, you are a brilliant conversationalist."

How's that for a definition? Corny? Sure. But true, isn't it? For instance applied to everyday encounters, the adage would work something like this: *Talk about the other person's interests, and ask questions.*

1. **Base these queries on what you see or already know about that person.** For example, Patti was sunning herself beside the playground pool. A fellow she had not seen before swam toward her. Before he flip-turned, Patti called, "Where'd you get those shoulder muscles?"

"Left over from when I was a kid," the young man shouted back as he swam away. At the end of the next lap, he jumped out of the pool, right at Patti's feet. "I'm Burt Bendell," he said. "I don't know you, do I?"

"Patti Palon," she replied. "But I'm serious. Do you lift weights or swim on a team or what?"

That was the beginning of a new friendship. The chemistry was there, to be sure. But the direction of the conversation was right, too. Patti knew her verbal interest in Burt was a pretty sure "come-hither."

2.   **In asking questions, do not pry, though, or get too personal.** Use open-ended questions to keep the conversation going. For example:

> Would you mind explaining further?
> How do you feel about this?
> What's your opinion?
> Can you give examples?

3.   **While talking and listening, keep direct eye contact.** Shifty eyes scanning your surroundings say: "I'm not really interested in what you are saying. I'm tolerating you until someone better comes along." Eye contact lends credence to your words.

4.   **If you do talk about a third person — someone who isn't with you at the time — edit what you say.** Be kind. Be truthful, telling the story exactly as it was told to you — and say from whom you heard it. Repeat only what you would say in the presence of the person about whom you are talking.

5.   **Listen carefully.** Conversation is two-way communication. Listening techniques are discussed on page 37.

6.   **Making the other person feel important is the apex of brilliant conversation.**

Fortunately, you can practice conversation every day. For instance, there's that fellow you have a crush on. You see him in the cafeteria during fifth period. He doesn't even know you exist, but you're dying to talk with him. Do your homework. Find out from his friends what he likes: sports? politics? data processing? math? Check his record in the school yearbook. Get a copy of his daily schedule from the school office. (One of the student office aides will help you.) His homeroom number will be on the card, too.

Casually pass his locker before school, and if you find him alone, stop. Introduce yourself. Tell him you heard he's a terrific swimmer — or that he backpacked in Mexico last summer — or whatever you did find out about him. And if you have boned up on the subject enough to ask intelligent questions, you are started on a good conversation, more than likely.

Or let's say you're ushering in church on Sunday morning. In walks a tall, willowy girl, haloed with golden hair. "Are you a visitor?" you ask as you guide her to an empty pew. She smiles and nods.

You rush back to the visitors' registry and discover her name is Susan Slater. She's from Chicago. After church, you introduce yourself: "Susan, I'm Jeff Pitt."

"How did you know my name?" she asks. You tell her, then ask about Chicago. With this start, you listen for tidbits of information from Susan. Or offer your own. For example, tell Susan about your Youth Fellowship meeting and ask her if she would like to come. If she shows interest, you may have a common concern. You may want to offer her a ride to the meeting.

The key to a two-way conversation is to listen for the other person's cues. Then relate them to your own life. Of course, you drop cues, too, which you hope the other person will pick up.

CROSS-COUNTRY SKI

If the cross-country skiing bug hasn't caught you, try it. Even 4-year-olds are doing it. It's a fun activity that you can share with peers or family in parks or back country. You will need the following equipment — borrowed, rented or bought:

1. **Cross-country boots.** Soles extend beyond the boot in order to slip under the toehold on a cable binding or into the clip closure of a pin binding. Most boots have synthetic-coated uppers that come slightly above the ankle. Some boots are fleece-lined. Leather boots are very expensive.

2. **Bindings.** Cross-country ski bindings hold the toe secure while the heel lifts and falls freely. Pin bindings are the most popular. They are metal toe plates into which boot toes are clamped securely. Pins are on the front of the plates. They fit into holes in the cross-country boot soles.

3. **Poles. Touring poles should be armpit-high.** The shaft is made of fiberglass or cane, and has a metal tip, hand strap and light plastic pole basket.

4. **Skis.** No-wax skis are better for beginners. The bottoms are molded into patterns to help you going uphill, as well as down. Waxed-bottom skis are what you use after you get experienced. When you apply the correct wax, you can glide uphill without slipping backwards. The type of wax used depends on outdoor temperatures and snow conditions. Use hard wax for temperatures below freezing. Waxed skis come in wood or fiberglass.

GO DUTCH TREAT FOR DINING OUT

"Separate checks, please," you announce to the waiter *before* you order. This paying your own way — referred to as "Dutch treat" by some people — is a teen-ager's boon. Fellows don't have to pay for two (as their fathers did). You don't have to date to eat out with peers. You can eat out in style (not fast food) with gourmet groups.

A Dutch treat gourmet group proceeds as follows: One of you acts as host or hostess for the event. He or she makes reservations; gets menus and prices in advance; collects money, including tax and tips; presides at the party; and pays the bill, which is all on one check. A more flexible plan, though, is for each of you to order and pay your own check, regardless of how many are in your party.

Bryce, Ellen, Kim and Tim have a Dutch treat group. "We started six months ago and pay $3 a week into a common fund. Then once a month we dine out," Tim explained. "In style! In the meantime, we read restaurant reviews and weekend ads. We figure this fancy fare gives us social savvy."

Tim was only half joking, while making a legitimate point. Dutch treats *do* add savvy — ease, know-how and confidence — in the social act of dining out.

EXPERIMENT WITH ESP
(EXTRASENSORY PERCEPTION)

Like most teen-agers, you probably have psychic urges, don't you? Then why not get together with your friends to explore your ESP?

One of many exciting books on the subject is *How to Test and Develop Your ESP*, by Paul Huson (Stein and Day Publishers, New York). Huson says you do not have to understand ESP to experiment with it. He offers several experiments for you to try, none of which takes specialized equipment.

He starts with J.B. Rine's famous deck of ESP cards — designed especially to test your ESP — that has been around since the 1930s. Five sets of decorated symbols are in this deck: circle, star, square, cross and wavy lines. You can make these designs on index cards for your own experimentation.

As one person turns over a card, another person, preferably in another room, calls out what symbol is on the card. Anyone who gets only five or less right does not score. That many good guesses can come up by chance. Any that are correct above five, though, indicate you may have ESP.

One test is merely a demonstration. You need quantity testing to determine results. But the fun is there even with a single try. For instance, two students in a demonstration-discussion on ESP used the Rine cards as an example. One of their classmates called out 10 of the 25 cards correctly. This supposedly indicated she had a high degree of ESP, the demonstrators explained.

Another of Huson's proposed experiments, which the two young men tried out in the classroom, proved a friend's ESP to be an hilarious dud. They asked Stash to hold a sealed envelope that contained a cut-out magazine picture. Then they instructed Ted to draw what he saw in his mind's eye as being the picture in the sealed envelope.

If Ted had ESP, the demonstrators explained, his drawing would resemble the picture in the sealed envelope. Ted's ESP, though, didn't work. He drew a picture of a tree. The envelope contained one of an Olympic swimmer. The class bell cut off any further experiments, but the kids are still talking about that neat ESP show.

ESP is going on all the time. So tune in on your own. Write down your uncanny experiences, such as picking up the phone to call a friend and having him on the line even before you dial his number. Note your flashes of intuition that prove right, such as cramming for a pop quiz you *feel* the teacher will spring on you the next day. She does!

FLY A KITE

"Go fly a kite" is more than an expression to rid yourself of a pesky kibitzer. In Japan, for instance, you might be taken literally, for there, almost everyone has a kite.

Once a year, in fact, crowds from Tokyo converge at the Oji Inari Shrine to toss away their old kites and to buy new ones to fly for the next year. Originating with the Shinto religion, this event now draws anyone who loves kites, color and excitement. Of course, the hawkers are there with thousands of bright kites, all shapes, sizes and prices. Some are tiny, hand-painted kites, the size of a deck of cards — flyable, though most people use them for decoration. One of the biggest models is the worm kite, which takes a team to fly. Costs range from a dollar to $150.

The idea of this traditional Japanese celebration could seed a kite fair among your own peers. Not that you need hawkers to sell kites. But you could converge on the nearest park, away from electric wires and too many trees.

Have yourselves a kite-flying day. Pick the right time of year, though. March winds on a spring-like day make the perfect climate. In fact, you would probably do well to allow this to be a more or less spontaneous day.

Talk it up. Give the event advance notice so everyone will have a kite. But save the exact day until the wind is right. And even if you don't plan a celebration, you will find one of sorts, already in progress on a balmy, breezy spring day.

Travel to any wide-open recreation area. There you will find plenty of company for your kite: box kites, not unlike the one invented by Lawrence Hargrave in 1893; the tetrahedral, like the one used by Alexander Graham Bell; and the usual cheaper editions, bearing advertising and cartoon figures. All will be darting, diving, climbing from strings fed out by teen-agers or daddies with their children, who will be draped on hillsides or running through meadows. You will have lots of action when the wind is companionable.

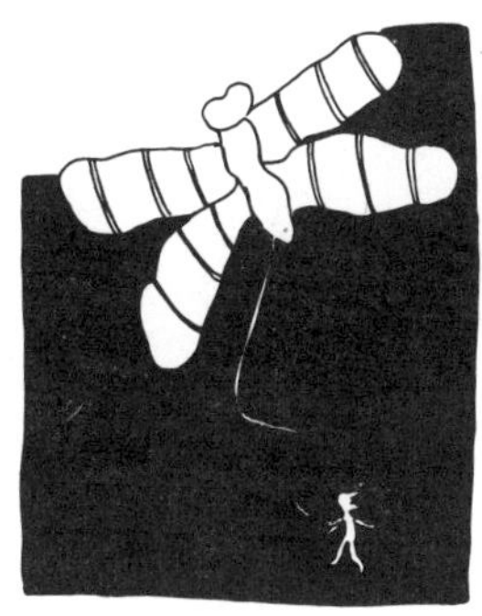

HOLD A BOX SOCIAL

Box socials are full of intrigue, disguise, surprise. At the turn of the century, they were a way of meeting new people, getting dates and breaking up "steadies" for an evening. At the same time, they were a source of revenue for club, church or school.

Today, box socials are still money-makers. Someone paid high stakes to eat with Dizzy Gillespie, for instance. His box lunch sold for hundreds of dollars, which helped finance the Pittsburgh Wind Symphony's Sunday Afternoon in the Park series. You, too, can raise money for church or charity — or simply have a different kind of party, using play money for bids. Here's how:

1. **Ask all girls (or all boys) to pack a lunch for two in a decorated box.** Instruct them to use nothing that will identify whose box it is. Suggest that boxes be brought in other boxes or sacks so no one will see what will be auctioned until the boxes are up for bids.

2. **Find a loud-voiced, enthusiastic peer who knows the auctioneering babble.**

3. **Make sure you have enough guests with boxes to match the eager bidders of the opposite sex, and vice versa.** In the case of too many boxes, let those who have already bid highest on a box bid again. The bidder may have two partners and a double lunch. Prepare extra box lunches in advance if you anticipate more bidders to be present than guests bringing boxes.

4. **The party excitement depends on frenzied bidding.** The auctioneer sets the pace. Planted bids will get action started. Hints and guesses as to contents and owners of the boxes raise the ante.

   A box social wraps up entertainment and refreshments in one package. And it's an activity that can make money for a worthy cause.

HAVE A BRIDAL GOWN
FASHION SHOW PARTY

For a change from blue jeans, try a fashion show of wedding gowns, past and near-present. Make it your main attraction for the next gang get-together. Initiate the idea for your church youth group. Put on a special performance for parents and relatives who have donated the gowns. Have a public showing to raise money for club, church or charities.

1.   Ask your acquaintances to resurrect the wedding gowns of someone in the family or neighborhood.

2.   Choose a drama-oriented friend to be commentator.

3.   Compose the script yourself or choose someone who has a flair for words.

Get detailed descriptions of each gown to be shown. The donor will likely be ready with names of fabric, trimming and accessories. If not, go to a bride's book or history of fashions and read up on language used for different periods, such as: sweetheart neckline; butterfly sleeves; tulle and lace; brown-plush bustled dress with buttons down the front, exquisite tucks, flounces and trim (dating back to your great-grandmother's time); above the knee, eggshell georgette with low waist (from the flapper years — your grandmother's, perhaps?); white satin, bias-cut, floor-length gown with cowl neckline (features of the 30s); lace over-skirt panels, covering yards and yards of white organdy, shirred at the waist (describes the early 60s).

Along with dress descriptions, get the names of the original owners, time and place the dresses were worn and relationship to any of the young people helping with the show.

4.   If the gown fits the recruiter, have her model it.
Otherwise, find someone who is the right size. Seams split easily on old dresses, so use models who are smaller than the dresses.

Handle all garments with tender loving care. Some may be priceless to the owners.

5. **Provide proper wedding music as background to the commentary.** If you have a piano and pianist, get copies of the wedding marches. Recordings will work as well — especially if you make your own tape in advance. For transitions and intermissions, use your own soloists and instrumentalists. But keep it as professional as possible, provided you go beyond the peer party stage.

6. **For your first performance, invite friends who won't boo or heckle too much.** Explain in advance that you want this event to be quite formal, since weddings are serious business, and each dress to be modeled represents a solemn occasion in the past. To help create a formal response, why not issue invitations that parody a real wedding?

7. **Serve wedding cakes for refreshments.**
You might even have someone demonstrate the proper way to cut the cake. You can also copy other reception routines, if you wish.

Your youth audience will enjoy most the novelty of seeing their friends in wedding finery. The dresses will draw secondary interest.

If you repeat your fashion show for parents, neighbors or any adult group, the tables will turn. The wedding gowns will arouse nostalgia in them. And they will love you for sharing the finery.

Once you have developed a successful performance, you may want to repeat it at nursing homes, senior citizens' clubs and adult Sunday school class parties. At least an abbreviated version is worth your time. The pleasure you will be giving others is the real payoff.

HAVE A CANDY PULL

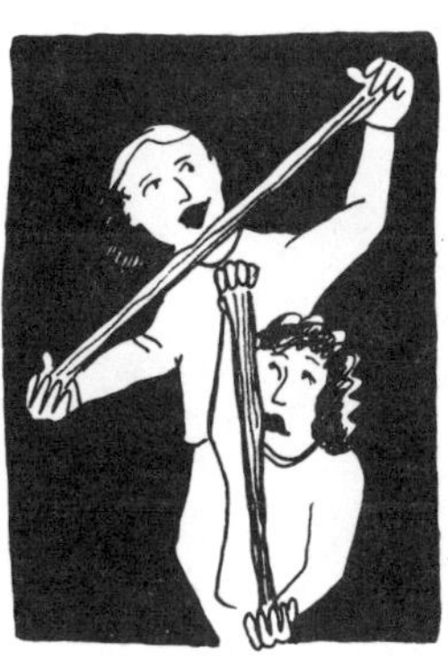

An old-fashioned candy pull is in season any time of the year, but especially during the holidays. Then you can make your own candy canes.

Any taffy recipe will guarantee a sticky, fun time, whether or not the candy hardens. You will need a big space with a floor that cleans easily. Taffy has a way of landing anywhere. That's because some people's hands are so warm that they never succeed in getting the taffy pulled hard enough to clip off with scissors. They enjoy pulling, nevertheless.

After following taffy recipe directions through the boiling stage, the actual pulling goes something like this:

1. **Take the mixture from the stove and pour it into several well-buttered plates.**

2. **Let the mixture cool until its edges lift easily and you can handle the warm, gooey glob.**

3. **Make sure your hands are clean and well-buttered.**

4. **Pull until you are tired, and pass the candy on to another person.**

5. **Rebutter your hands and retrieve what you gave away.**

6. **Keep on pulling until the rope of candy is hard enough to snip.**

7. **Cut off one-inch pieces or six-inch sticks.** At this point, the taffy will become brittle.

To make candy canes, you vary the routine slightly:

1. **After you remove the boiled mixture from the stove, color one batch red, and the other green.**

2. **When two of you with different-colored taffy have pulled the candy to the hardening stage, quickly twist one colored rope around the other rope.**

3. **Clip to cane length, and curve the top of each stick as it lies on the plate, before it completely hardens.** These make tasty Christmas tree decorations.

HAVE A CLOWN PARTY

This is a double-barrel party. Your invited peer guests are the clowns. Neighborhood kids and their parents are the audience. Both groups have fun interacting. Party preparations include the following:

1. **Collect a stack of old clothes for teen guests to paw through and piece together for clown suits.**

2. **Provide plenty of pins, string, tape, scissors, needles and thread for makeshift put-togethers.**

3. **In an area well-protected from the expected spilled grease, provide makeup:** vegetable oil or cold cream, cotton-tipped skewers (toothpicks will do), tissues and grease paint or odds and ends of an everyday makeup.

4. **Provide plenty of properties to trigger ideas for clown acts,** such as: baby carriages, a ladder, stilts, a rubber hose, a broom, toys, old picture frames without pictures or glass, gunnysacks, pans and a broken chair.

5. **Invite parents and children to your proposed impromptu parade and show.**

6. **As your friends arrive, encourage them to start making themselves up as clowns.** Explain that real clowns each have their own copyrighted face, that no one apes another's. Announce that prizes will be given for the most unusual, the funniest and the saddest faces. Also explain to your clowns that you have provided an audience to see their acts.

7. **Encourage each to put on an act, either during the parade or in the circus arena (wherever your party is held).** Suggest that they may help each other or work directly with their audience. Encourage one idea from each, if possible. You will be amazed at the variety of acts your friends will spontaneously create once they are behind clown faces. The shyest person may become your funniest clown.

8. **When all faces and costumes are ready (or at a specified time), start your parade and show.** Weather permitting, parade down your street. This will be the signal for the neighbors to join the party. They may tag behind the clowns back to your yard.

   Perform in a single ring.

9. **After the acts, award the prizes.** You promised awards for saddest, funniest and most unusual. Also give booby prizes — for anything, such as messiest, quietest, noisiest, tallest, shortest, slowest. Try to award something to each performer.

10. **Give the audience treats, too.** Let the clowns pass out inflated balloons. Peddle popcorn, ice cream on sticks, spun sugar and/or peanuts in the shell. Have yourself a real live circus in your own backyard!

EXCHANGE WHITE ELEPHANTS

White elephants are items, old or new, which you no longer use — or never have. You can disguise them as the following: door prizes, surprise birthday gifts, articles to be auctioned off to raise money or gifts to be exchanged at parties. For a white elephant party, here are some suggestions:

1. **Write invitations on white elephant cut-outs.**
   Ask each guest to bring something he or she is willing to give away. It might be that purple sweater that never fit, a duplicate record or tape of a popular song, a whistle cord you braided at camp when you were 10 or your outgrown jeans.

2. **Suggest that white elephants be wrapped to look as if they were store-bought.** Collect the white elephants at the door as your guests arrive. Number each package. At the same time, give each person another number (not the one on his or her original package).

   At the time of the gift exchange, call out the number on each package and match with guests' numbers. Mismatching of presents with people becomes hilarious. Allow exchanges *before* packages are unwrapped, to add speculation to the activity.

3. **Another white elephant party idea is to auction off the wrapped presents that guests bring with them.** Use play money or IOU papers. Either have one person be an auctioneer, or have each guest auction off his or her own white elephant. The fun is in the bidding. And the liveliness of the auctioning makes the party successful.

MAKE HOMEMADE ICE CREAM

In one of the West Virginia Folk Festival tents, a dozen young men crank five-gallon freezers of ice cream. As fast as they freeze it, buyers grab up cones and buckets of the smooth, velvety frozen cream. That's because it is homemade, like no commercial brand.

This "feat and sweet" is a sure teen-age tantalizer. Hand-cranking challenges brawn. And almost everyone likes ice cream.

1. First, you need a freezer or two.
These non-electrical ones still show up at flea markets, garage and rummage sales. Some hardware supermarkets have them in stock. Secondhand stores and junkyards may have them. Check out attics and basements of great-grandparents and older neighbors. Or have a scavenger hunt with a hand-cranked ice cream freezer (in working condition) as one of the objects to find.

2. An ice cream recipe is next.
Perhaps you have a family hand-me-down — a cooked custard, rich in calories. Here is a recipe recommended by a modern dentist because it has no chemical additives or refined sugar:

> 9 eggs
> 1½ quarts heavy whipping cream
> 1 teaspoon salt
> 3-4 tablespoons pure vanilla, according to taste
> 1 teaspoon peppermint flavoring (no imitations)
> 1 small ripe avocado (adds thickening)
> ½ - ¾ cup of honey, according to taste
>
> Mix all the above ingredients in a blender until thick and smooth. Pour into the ice cream freezer and crank until hard. This makes about 5 quarts. Variations may include adding fresh fruit. If you plan to add nuts, decrease vanilla to 1 tablespoon and add 3 tablespoons maple flavoring. After blending, add 1 cup chopped pecans.

3. **Ice and rock salt are necessary for freezing.**
   After pouring the ice cream mixture in the cylinder, insert the wooden paddles, screw on the top, place the cylinder inside the bucket and pack the bucket with layers of salt and ice. Secure the top apparatus with the crank, and start turning. As the ice melts, add more salt and ice.

4. **Take turns cranking to provide the power.**
   Offer awards to the most energetic crankers — like licking the paddles. Or get everyone in the act with at least 10 turns of the crank apiece.

5. **Serve equal portions in cold dishes.**

HAVE A PANCAKE PARTY

Instead of meeting at the pizza parlor after a football or basketball game, invite the crowd to your home for pancakes (with your parents' permission, of course). You can handle this mass production, in spite of high food costs, by following one of three procedures:

1. **Charge a set price** to help defray expenses. Why not? Your friends spend plenty for after-game food they consume at their favorite drive-ins or fast food hang-outs. Besides, an admission fee discourages uninvited guests who invade parties like red ants at a picnic.

2. **Ask your friends to contribute the ingredients:** pancake mix, butter, syrup, sausage or bacon. Have everything brought in ahead of time, however, to make certain you have all the necessities.

3. **Buy all ingredients yourself and equalize the cost among the consumers.** Add your bill before the party. Divide by the number of kids who show. Collect while they are still eating.

From your guest list, choose experienced "flippers" to toss the pancakes. Add to their fun by crowning them with makeshift chefs' caps. Possibly, other guests can quickly make these chef symbols out of newspapers or scrap materials at the party.

Be informal. Serve directly from the skillet. Let guests sit where they will — on the floor, likely, when table space is taken. Don't worry about space. Think of the number of teen-agers who can squeeze into a single car.

The homemade pancake party is a choice variation of the routine after-game togetherness. Beware, though. It may become a *Guinness Book of World Records* party, as Sue's almost did. After a match for which he had lost 10 pounds to qualify, a wrestler made up for his fasting. He downed 20 pancakes and challenged his buddies to beat his record.

Maybe in such cases you will want to charge by the pancake. Or is the cost of the exhibition worth the entertainment it provides?

HOLD A PROGRESSIVE BOARD GAME PARTY

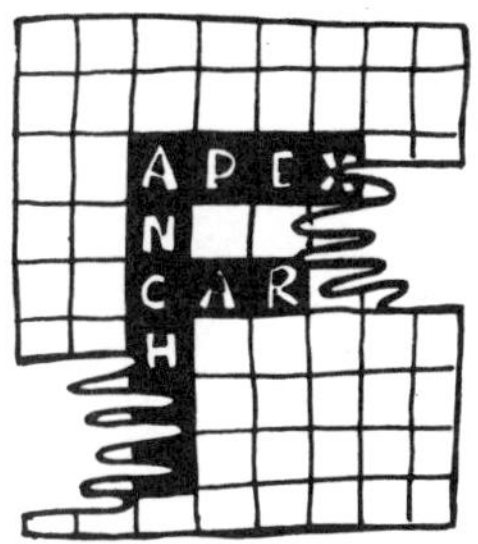

You probably own some of the traditional board games that have a cardboard field and movable pieces like letter cubes. So drag these out of hiding and have yourself a progressive board game party — with the help of your friends and their boards.

The progression and games used can vary. But here is a sample procedure you may want to follow:

1. **Assemble as many games as you will need for the number of guests you invite.** Include such games as Scrabble, Boggle, Mastermind, Perquackery and Backgammon, or whatever is popular at the moment.

2. **Solicit volunteers who are willing to entertain for one of these games in their recreation room, garage, porch or on their lawn.**

3. **Coordinate boards and entertainment sites.**
The number of guests will determine how many tables of a single game will be at each house.

4. **Ask guests to congregate at a central location.**
From there, fan out to the various homes after each person draws a number and game. For example, those drawing Backgammon will head for one place; Scrabble, another.

5. **Avoid having too many playing a single board.**
Mobility and sociability are more important to the success than winning the games.

6. **As each game ends, half of the players move on to the next location for another board game, with the other half remaining at that site.** The number of moves will depend on the length of the games, of course. Don't worry about one game ending before another. Although this will happen, your guests will enjoy the interludes. In fact, the whole concept of progression is a "fruit basket tip-over" mixer.

7. **You may plan to meet again at your starting point at the conclusion of the games.** Either serve refreshments then, or progress the snacks along with the games.

8. **A progressive party can also be held under one roof, provided you have enough rooms.** Follow the same routine, only set up a different game in each of several rooms. This plan unites the party more. Transportation from place to place is eliminated, but so is the variety of locale. Hence, the best progression is from house to house, within walking distance. That way, the sharing of responsibilities and expenses makes the party easier to repeat another time.

HAVE A ROARING '20s PARTY

The idea hatched when the American history teacher gave extra grade credit points to students who dressed in 1920s styles or could identify the lyrics to "Yes, We Have No Bananas Today." The juniors caught the spirit and organized a Roaring '20s party. And they figured it's well worth copying. Here, then, are some of the things they did to identify the party with the era:

1. **They dressed according to the period.**
   Boys wore straw boaters (hats). Girls wore headache bands (strips of ribbon tied around the forehead). Some wore authentic costumes of the period, borrowed from relatives' attics — Grandma's wedding dress (up to the knees in front, trailing in the back) or Great-uncle's racoon coat.

2. **Music created the excitement of the '20s.**
   Several dappers (boys) strummed borrowed ukuleles. The whole gang sang "Yes, Sir, She's My Baby." Song sheets were distributed so that everyone had the words for singing popular hits of that day: "Down by the Old Mill Stream," "Moonlight Bay" and "In a Little Spanish Town." An old-fashioned victrola blared out oldies. Flappers danced the Charleston.

HAVE A SHOW-AND-TELL PARTY

Remember when you had a chance to show off your new shoes, your favorite toy, that pretty pebble you picked up on the way to school? That was back in kindergarten, of course.

The same activity — show and tell — is fun for teen-agers, too, since almost everyone likes to be the center of attention once in a while. And this activity guarantees you a momentary place in the sun. As a party idea, it also provides a whole evening's entertainment.

1. **When you invite your guests, ask each one to bring something to show and discuss.** If anyone asks for suggestions, here are samples of past performances:

    - A high-school star quarterback showed bronzed baby shoes and his football shoes. "So you can see how I've grown," he said. Then he described last Saturday's game, as seen from a quarterback's point of view.

    - A young hunter brought his bow and arrow — the bow he used to kill his first deer. He described the experience in detail.

    - A recent Washington, D.C., visitor exhibited a six-inch model of the Washington Monument and verbally portrayed the view she saw from the top of that historic site.

    - A young man held a camp song book as he told about the campfire singing at his church camp. Then he led the group in a couple of songs from the book.

    - Two young women came to the party dressed in clown makeup and clothes. They presented an acrobatic act similar to what they put on at veterans' hospitals as part of a clown ministry.

2. **At the party, have each guest draw a number so you can determine the order of presentation.** You may prefer to call for volunteers first. Follow with numbers of those who have not performed.

3. **Designate a maximum time limit, or someone may take over the entire evening.** Such a situation would spoil the show-and-tell concept completely. The success of your party depends on everyone taking part.

4. **For refreshments, use show and tell, too.**
    Involve one of your friends who works for a fast-food franchise, for instance. Have him or her dress in an employee's cap or uniform and describe the making of a hamburger or pizza. Follow up with samples for everyone.

    Or if one of your friends bakes well, have him or her wear a chef's cap and apron, display baking utensils and give the recipe for the cake, cookies or other dessert that you will share with the group.

You can anticipate all sorts of surprises and fun at a show-and-tell party. Simply provide space and alert your friends. They will do the rest.

GO SKATEBOARDING

Skateboarding is a passion for Steve, as he demonstrated before his public-speaking class in high school. His enthusiasm was catching. "Skateboarding demands physical agility and courage," Steve challenged his classmates.

Complete with helmet, gloves, tennis shoes and elbow and knee pads, he rode down the aisle of the classroom on his skateboard, maneuvered quick turns and made a complete stop. This unexpected activity both shocked and fascinated his teen-aged audience.

"The most prevalent problem is safety," Steve continued. "Wearing safety equipment like what I have on is very important. Especially the helmet.

"The Consumer Product Safety Commission has come out with some terrifying figures: 'One-third of all accident victims are beginners. One-third of all accidents occur when the skateboard strikes irregularities on the skating surface.'

"The commission recommends that skateboards be used in controlled environments specifically intended for skateboarding. That means not using public streets or sidewalks. Until our City Commission's plans for a skateboard park go through, we should skate only on school or church parking lots — when no cars are there, of course."

Steve then showed the class the way to fall so as to prevent fracturing the lower arm. He also wrote the following information on the chalkboard:

HIA Hazard Report — Skateboards
Superintendent of Documents
U.S. Government Printing Office
Washington, D.C. 20402
Report No. 052-011-00175-9

During the forum which followed, Steve answered three questions:

1.   When did skateboarding start?
"In the '60s. The first were 2x4s attached to roller skates. Gradually, they got more sophisticated. But it wasn't until 1972 that skateboards really advanced."

2.   Why then?
"Urethane wheels. They make the difference. They give grip, stability and speed for doing tricks."

3.   How long did it take Steve to get to be really good on his skateboard? "About a year. I've had plenty of practice and my coordination is pretty good — that's important."

Steve's demonstration and explanation turned out to be a recruiting speech. Four of the fellows in the class later tried riding his skateboard in the church parking lot. Now they have their own boards and meet on Saturdays. They think this is terrific exercise. And they have fun together.

START A RAP GROUP

A rap is an informal talk session among your peers. You hash out problems, share joys and and frustrations and air situations you feel you need help in solving. Raps are fun, too.

Sara Leonard rapped regularly with friends from her church youth group, until she moved to another city. She says she misses the rap comradeship and hopes to start another group in her new location. "As soon as I'm better acquainted," she adds.

When asked what's so special about a rap group, she explained, "You get feedback and emotional support. It's a neat way to give and take criticism that's honest, not faky. You understand your own problems better, too, once you find out the other kids have similar ones. I guess I'd say it's a sort of group therapy, without a psychologist present."

If you want to start a rap group, here are a few suggestions to help you launch it:

1. **Invite a half-dozen friends to your house.** Keep the number between six and eight.

2. **Lead the discussion yourself at this first get-together.** This will give you a chance to set the pattern and lay the ground rules.

3. **Encourage everyone to talk about what you all have in common.** Then you can explore ways of handling these concerns (like dating curfews, classroom cheating or trying to live up to your own ideals).

4. **At all future sessions, rotate leaders and locations so everyone gets in the act equally.**

5. **Abide by two honor-bound promises:** that you will be supportive of each other — truthful, without putting anyone down; and that all talk is confidential — no telling outsiders.

6. **If your rap sessions become petty, picky, "porny" or preachy, call it quits!** You've ruined a good thing. You may avoid such pitfalls by opening each session with a reminder of the original intents of honest feedback and emotional support.

    Even if you don't organize a rap group, a spontaneous rap session among friends has its benefits. It is especially a way of finding out how much you have in common with your peers. Sit on the living room floor, around a camp fire, in a ski lodge or on a sandy beach. Wherever, rap and enjoy!

TAPE-RECORD YOUR FRIENDS

Anyone with a tape recorder can turn a nothing-to-do evening into a happening.

1. **Divide your group into teams.**
   Allow 10-15 minutes for each unit to prepare a skit, song, interviews or individual acts. Call on each team to perform while you record.

2. **Emcee a talent show if you have enough extroverts present.** Introduce the acts without preparation time. Almost anyone responds to spontaneous taping. Hearing the play-back is exciting and personal. Everyone listens for his or her own voice.

3. **Ask questions of the group, such as:** what would you do if you knew exactly when you would die? Pass the mike from person to person. Let anyone who has an opinion record it. Save second comments until all have had a turn. Play back the answers.

4. **If this stimulates further discussion, try one of these questions:**

   > What if all food were in pill form?
   > What would you consider to be a teen-ager's utopia?
   > What if everyone were an only child?
   > What would you do differently if you were president of the United States?
   > Why are we here?

4. **Pattern your activity after television's "Tonight Show," or any other multiple-interview program.** Ask one of your friends to be talk show host. Have the others draw cards, on which you have written names of famous (or not-so-famous) people to be interviewed. Or half the group may draw advertisements to create or mimic, if your guests are many and you want to involve everyone). Proceed with the

show's regular format, role-playing the entire program.

5. Tape quiz shows.
Prepare questions and visual paraphernalia ahead of time. Some board games are adaptable to quiz recordings, such as "Go to the Head of the Class," or "Twenty Questions."

Once you have made a tape, the play-back also becomes entertainment for a year or two later — provided you can afford not to erase the tape. Something about hearing oneself holds unlimited fascination.

MORE THINGS TO DO TOGETHER:

Conduct a **sing-a-long.** Have an old-fashioned **spell-down.** Have more parties: a **lawn party,** a **pizza party,** a **winter sports party,** a **hayride** or **sleighride,** a **scavenger hunt,** a **treasure hunt,** a **pool party** with water games and races, a **kids' party** (play children's games) or a **2000 A.D. party.** Hold a **neighborhood track meet.** Hold a **prayer breakfast** in a park. **Pop corn.** Organize a **block party.** Put on a **hobby show.** Play **outdoor children's games.** Read a **play,** each one taking a part. Hold a **square** or **folk dance.** Start a **birthday club** that celebrates each member's birthday. Put on a **magic show. Gather around a camp fire** on the beach.

Give Yourself Away

BAND BIRDS

An Alfred Hitchcock movie, *The Birds*, may have scared the living daylights out of you during a late-night television showing. It was fictitious, of course, and grossly exaggerated. Nonetheless, birds *are* fantastic creatures, worth much more of your time than a two-hour movie scare. For instance:

- The ruby-throated hummingbird, which weighs only an eighth of an ounce, flies 500 miles across the Gulf of Mexico in 25 hours, while beating its wings 50 times a second.

- To prepare for their 2,700-mile non-stop flight over water to the shores of South America, some sandpipers eat enough to double their weight in three weeks.

- The Tennessee warbler migrates some 3,000 miles south each year. Then it often returns to the same tree where it nested the year before.

Scientific knowledge like this depends on volunteer bird-banders all over the world. Therefore, if these bird activities fascinate you, why don't you check into the bird-banding business?

You will discover that, among other things, each of the 2,000 licensed banders in the United States has a permit. The license is issued by the Fish and Wildlife Service. To get such a permit, you must be able to convince three experts that you can recognize common birds that live in or visit your area.

You can become one of the thousands of volunteers who help licensed banders record valuable scientific facts about the migration of birds, their habitats and habits.

Debby Joy did exactly that while she was camping at Martha's Vineyard one summer. She attached herself to a licensed sea gull-bander. Before her vacation ended, she had learned how to handle gulls at the seaside rookery. Ms. Hunt carefully supervised Debby's actions and recorded the data inscribed on tiny feather-weight bands attached to the birds' legs.

Whether or not you find a licensed bander to help, start your bird-banding activity by investing in one of the three most inclusive, up-to-date bird guides. Perhaps you are already familiar with that light green hardback, *Peterson's Field Guide* (small enough to jam into your jeans' pocket). It was published originally in 1934. Its author, Roger Tory Peterson — probably the most famous living ornithologist — has revised *Guide to Field Identification: Birds of North America* (Houghton Mifflin).

The Audobon Society Field Guide to the North American Birds (Knopf) is another favorite. And competing with those two is *Birds of North America*, published by Golden Press.

Armed with one of these identification books, you will soon recognize birds in your locale. And even if you never become a licensed bander, your environment will trill with *now-identifiable* bird songs and calls.

BE A CHURCH VOLUNTEER

For those of you who have church connections, your go-power, enthusiasm and sheer vitality are welcome resources in any religious organization. At the same time, all volunteer work you do is experience that counts on future résumés. And where can you find better proving grounds for getting along with people of all ages?

The following service activities are yours for the asking in most churches:

1.   Help in the church office.
Type letters. Update bulletin boards. Answer telephones. Fold and stuff envelopes for special mailings.

2.   Assist in the library.
Check out books. Catalog and repair books. Give book reviews. Conduct a children's story hour.

3. **Help in the church nursery.**
    Take care of babies and toddlers during Sunday morning worship services. Be available for special events, like family nights. Repair and collect toys and furnishings.

4. **Serve on dinner crews.**
    Prepare vegetables and salads. Decorate and set tables. Serve the dinner. Run the dishwasher.

5. **Help with church grounds maintenance.**
    Trim shrubbery. Edge walks. Rake leaves. Pick up papers.

6. **Assist with Vacation Bible School.**
    Tell stories. Teach arts and crafts. Take charge of recreation. Guide worship projects. Organize field trips. Prepare refreshments. Keep attendance records.

7. **Offer your services on Sundays as:** an acolyte, an usher, a greeter, an audio controller, a film projectionist, a junior church aide, a choir member, a bell-ringer (in the bell choir), a liturgist or an attendance-taker.

8. **Be an active member of youth church school class and fellowship (evening group).** Serve on committees. Accept offices. Recruit new members. Participate in projects and activities. Attend regularly.

9. **Tape-record church worship services and loan your tapes to shut-ins.**

10. **Baby-sit for members who are on official church business during the week.**

11. **Make posters for special events.**

12. **Design and embroider or paint liturgical banners.**

13. **Collect stamps, package them and send them to missionaries.** (They sell stamps for cash to finance special projects.)

14. **If you drive and have an autombile, offer to take someone who has no transportation to church services.**

15. **Be a church camp junior counselor.**
Teach or help with any sports skill you have. Help with singing, dramatics, Bible study, arts and crafts — whatever is your forte.

BE A COMMUNITY SERVICES VOLUNTEER

Discover what you *can* do, as well as what you *like* to do by serving your area in one or more of the cadet programs for youth.

1. **Resources for Youth programs are active across the nation.** Two of their effective projects are Youth Tutor Youth and Day Care Youth Helper Porgram.

2. **Work with rescue squads.**
Junior rescue workers are a vital part of many local units, which train high-school juniors and seniors.

Every talk Jon gave in speech class one semester was about Rescue Eight, the community emergency corps of which he is a junior member. He told how he spends three nights a week from 5 to 11 taking instruction, practicing and going on real emergency runs.

His experiences include helping victims of auto wrecks, fires and heart attacks. He knows paramedical procedures and can do anything a senior paramedic can do except drive the ambulance.

Judy, a high-school senior in another town, has even delivered a baby while on an ambulance run.

3.   Sheriff's departments have cadet programs, too.

Carolyn liked the first three months of taking calls in the office, observing arrests, filing reports. But one night, she took a rape phone call. After that, she quit. "I've had it," she said. "It's not for me."

Her friend, Marilyn, is still a cadet. She is even cruising with officers, going where the action is. She likes the work so well that she is applying for police training at the state law enforcement academy.

Whether or not you follow through these services to careers in them, you are serving others while training. The better programs also develop your initiative, industry and independence. And you can explore yourself and the world around you. Perhaps you will find commitment and self-direction. You will know only after being a cadet.

BE A VOLUNTEER FIREFIGHTER

"Do you like to chase fires? Then be a junior volunteer firefighter," Mitch challenged his classmates in a discussion on community activities.

"What do you do?" Pat asked.

"Basically, a junior trains to be a senior firefighter, who is also a volunteer. We go to the fires, help with the ladders, lay fire hose and wash down roads. The seniors call us go-fers. Go-fers go wherever needed. We aren't allowed to enter burning buildings, though. Nor are we allowed to drive the trucks or fight fires. I guess I'd say that at a fire, juniors work outside; seniors, inside."

Mitch said the fire hall is his second home. He even has mail sent there. He works every Thursday night, cleaning the hall. And once a month, he helps with the Friday night bingo party (to raise money for equipment).

"Suppose I want to be a junior firefighter. How do I become one?" asked Ted.

"Know someone who is. In my junior group, applicants are voted on by the members. If you get two blackballs, you aren't in. (That means two votes against you.) If you are voted down three times that way in the first meeting, you have another chance at the next one. If you don't make it then, you can apply again in six months."

"OK, but what are the requirements for membership?" Ted persisted.

"You have to be 18. You have to list all traffic offenses and arrests on your application. And you have to live in the fire district. Usually, you get voted in, unless you're a real jerk."

Phil then asked, "What training do they give you?"

"It covers all the trucks," Mitch said. "You have to memorize the trucks — what's in them, without looking."

Finally, one of the girls asked, "What are your parents' reactions to your being a junior firefighter?"

"Dad hates my getting up in the middle of the night to run to fires. But Mom likes it because it keeps me out of mischief," Mitch concluded.

Wherever fire departments are manned by volunteers, you likely will find a junior firefighter corps that has procedures similar to those Mitch shared with his friends. Call your local fire hall for further information, unless you know a junior firefighter. In that case, query him or her.

BE A HOSPITAL VOLUNTEER

Are you seriously thinking about a medical career? Doctor, nurse, technician, brain or heart surgeon — all are glamorized in television programs. But what's the *real* drama like? As a high-school student, you can find out for yourself while helping patients in hospitals. There are several programs open to both boys and girls:

1. **Candy-stripers are teen-age girls who belong to Future Nurses of America and devote designated hours of service to local hospitals.**

2. **Where FNA clubs do not exist, RN (registered nurse) organizations staff volunteer services.** These are organized within the hospital rather than in high school. An example of RN clubs that are hospital-contained is Teen-age Volunteers of Sarasota Memorial Hospital in Florida. There, an average of 55 volunteers gave 14,362 hours of service in a single year. They helped with patient care, therapy, admittance, x-ray and the hospitality shop and cart.

    RN club members (and candy-stripers) get tours of hospital facilities, opportunities to observe and help with patient care and exposure to various health-related occupations.

3. **The Boy Scouts of America also have hospital programs for young men who think they want to enter health care fields.**

4. **Likewise, hospitals have their own volunteer male nurse training to stimulate interest in this rapidly growing occupation.**

    If you are interested in one of these volunteer programs, contact your school nurse or nearest hospital. Nurses are no longer one gender.

VOLUNTEER TO HELP
THE MENTALLY HANDICAPPED

"I've never been appreciated more in my life!" Judy said after her first visit to Marcy State Hospital (Pennsylvania). "You should see the welcome those almost-forgotten citizens give us — like little children anticipating Christmas."

Judy first visited an institution for retarded adults with her high-school child-care class. (They had expanded their studies to include these adults.) Following that field trip, each student worked for an hour or two a week (for nine weeks) with a mentally handicapped resident.

Judy asked to work with a non-verbal patient, and the results were fantastic. The resident assigned her had refused to do anything except watch television during his two years in the hospital. He would not speak, although he could. But in spite of this man's negative attitude, Judy had him laughing and talking by her third visit.

1. **Because these patients need individual attention, they come to life whenever they get it.**

2. **What do they respond to? Simple activities, such as:** doing exercises with someone; tossing a Nerf ball back and forth; learning how to bowl with plastic pins; and learning basic activities like counting money, sewing on buttons, writing the letters of the alphabet, drawing and painting or identifying traffic signal meanings. Also, you can guide them in simple crafts.

3. **Bringing your youth, vitality and personal touch add excitement and anticipation to mundane days for these mentally retarded patients — a challenge you may want to follow through.**

   If so, investigate the possibility that your church or school has ongoing programs for serving a state institution. Or call directly to the nearest state facility. Ask if they take high-school volunteers. Offer an hour or two of your time a week. And if the need is great, you may want to recruit members of your church youth group to go with you.

HELP WITH SPECIAL OLYMPICS FOR THE MENTALLY HANDICAPPED

Sign up, the next time you hear an announcement over your high-school public address system, pleading for volunteers to help man special olympics.

Without people like you, these happy events could not continue. Each tournament needs 100-200 volunteers to serve as officials, announcers and "huggers," stationed at finish lines to congratulate the participants.

Once a year, the mentally retarded compete in these special olympics at various sites throughout the United States. A runner carries the symbolic torch. Athletes march in the traditional opening parade. But track and field events are modified, of course. And everyone wins.

Each participant gets a ribbon for entering an event. Each receives another for finishing. At designated official Special Olympics area meets, gold medalists qualify for state competition.

If you volunteer, you may have to report to a nearby college or university athletic field, since these are popular sites for the games. Health and physical education departments of these schools sponsor the events. City park departments assist or sponsor. And the Joseph P. Kennedy Foundation contributes funds.

Are you interested? "If you could have seen their faces up there on the victory stands — they had the greatest time," reported one volunteer after the Dyche Stadium meet at Northwestern University. "All participants were winners. And we were, too."

BE KIND TO PARENTS

For one day, why not put your parents first on your agenda? Do what they ask you to do. Go where they want you to go. Be kind.

Communicate. Listen. Stop making excuses, complaining or saying, "I'll do it later."

Tell them you love them. Show your approval of them. Compliment. Appreciate.

1. **Take the initiative by thinking ahead of them as to what you can do to help them:** take care of baby sister? mow the lawn? wash the car? run errands?

2. **List all the things you can recall that your parents *expect* you to do.**

3. **Then list extras that you can do for them above and beyond what they ask or suggest.**

4. **From these two lists, start doing the most important item and work off as many as you can in one day.**

Will your mother and dad catch on to your Parent's Day idea? Why not? You are giving your best attitude, response and physical energy. They will quickly wise up that something is special. If they don't, you aren't trying hard enough to please.

Don't tell, though. *Let your good works* speak for themselves. And your reward? Or course, there will be one — that exhilarating feeling which comes from being extra kind, patient and giving.

BE NEIGHBORLY

Teen-agers are the focal point of a neighborhood. The smaller kids become your clones. Parents worry about you. And older adults watch your every move.

In this center-stage position, you can act out all kinds of plots — comedy or tragedy. Here and now, though, let's consider the "happy ending" ones — sitcoms that will add vitality to your block or community.

These are projects you can initiate:

1. **Collect used magazines and books.**
    Distribute them to institutions that will accept them eagerly, such as veterans' hospitals, libraries, rest homes, children's homes and wards in hospitals and schools.

2. **Play Santa Claus at Christmas time** with neighbors' help. Get names of needy families from agencies. Buy or collect gifts to match the children's ages. Wrap and place the gifts in a big sack. Dress up in a Santa suit and deliver gifts.

3. **Play board games with elderly neighbors** who like checkers, chess, Monopoly or Scrabble.

4. **Celebrate the birthdays of older neighbors, especially if their families are elsewhere.** Have a party. Bake a cake. At least telephone or send a card.

5. **Shovel a path after an early-morning snowstorm — before your neighbor is up.** His or her surprise will keep a halo around your head for a long time.

6. **If you like to take pictures, show your slides or movies for older neighbors in their homes.** Keep your show short, though. Be both commentator and projectionist, bringing your own equipment.

7. **Sit with a shut-in for an hour or two, to give the relative a break from constant watch.** Read aloud. Write letters. Chat about your teen-age activities. Listen to stories of the past.

8. **Occasionally, plan something special for the neighborhood kids,** whether or not you have younger brothers and sisters. Show slides or home movies. Hold a hand puppet or talent show, with the children participating. Play your guitar, sax or harmonica and have a sing-along.

9. **Organize a group to sing Christmas carols from door to door.**

10. **Publish a neighborhood newsletter.**

That kid next door (you) can be a real asset!

CLEAN UP LOCAL PARKS AND STREAMS

American communities have spring-cleanings. This is the time they seek volunteers to clean up parks, boulevards and waterways. Usually, they welcome extra help in the fall, too. Therefore, you have a service opportunity almost at your front door.

Why not offer to pick up trash, pull weeds, rake leaves, cut out deadwood? Better yet, organize a crew of teen-agers to put in a day's work.

1. **First, contact the city government — whoever is in command.** Get permission.

2. **Then organize crews of classmates to work a given area on a designated Saturday.**

3. **Round up equipment,** such as trucks to carry away rubbish, and rakes, mowers and pruning shears.

4. **On the big day, assemble at a central spot early in the morning and then fan out to various work areas.**

5. **Ask crew captains to report back at the end of the day as to the amount of ground covered** (for publicity purposes).

6. **Enlist Future Homemakers of America (or another such group) to prepare a picnic lunch, at cost.** Have everyone eat together at the same time. This will give a sense

of unity and add fun.

Ask adults to help, too. They need your vision and enthusiasm to get them started on civic clean-ups. These activities will build youth-adult relationships.

COLLECT OLD CLOTHES FOR CHARITY BOXES

Do you have a closet loaded with clothes you have outgrown or never wear? You're not sentimental about *all* that clutter, are you?

1. **Then give away some of it to charities:** Salvation Army, Goodwill Industries, Catholic Charities, Church World Service, you name it. They all desperately need your cast-offs for their local services and around-the-world concerns.

   Many of these charities provide deposit bins in shopping centers. Take your items there. Telephone the agency directly, and someone there will send a truck to pick up your contributions.

2. **While in this charitable spirit, why not telephone your neighbors for their give-aways?** Tell them you will take their old clothes to the deposit centers, along with yours. You will be doing them, as well as the charities, a favor.

3. **Before giving your stuff away, though, make a list of the items and their approximate value.** Keep this information. Your parents may find it useful at income tax time, when they are looking for charitable deductions.

   By using this system of cleaning out your closet, you are helping yourself, your parents, your neighbors and your community. How's that for one big scoop?

CRUSADE FOR A CAUSE

A cause is any project or service that obsesses you.

Sixteen-year-old Alda's cause, for instance, is animal rights. Her latest crusade is passing out petitions to make the wolf the national mammal. She has also raised money to pay for a television commercial discouraging the use of animal furs for coats. The national organization, called Fund for Animals, provided Alda with buttons and T-shirts to sell. On the shirts she has imprinted: "Real People Wear Fake Furs." Alda is a girl with a cause that helps and preserves.

Your cause may be one of several, such as: cleaning up a local stream; petitioning for a youth center; trying to get a teen-ager on the school board; curbing your town or city's air pollution; getting a teen-agers' talk show on a local radio station; initiation or expanding a city recreational program for children that hires teen-agers; organizing a summer camp for your local church; or starting a 4-H program in your school.

Whatever your cause, find something that consumes your time and energy *because it is worth it!*

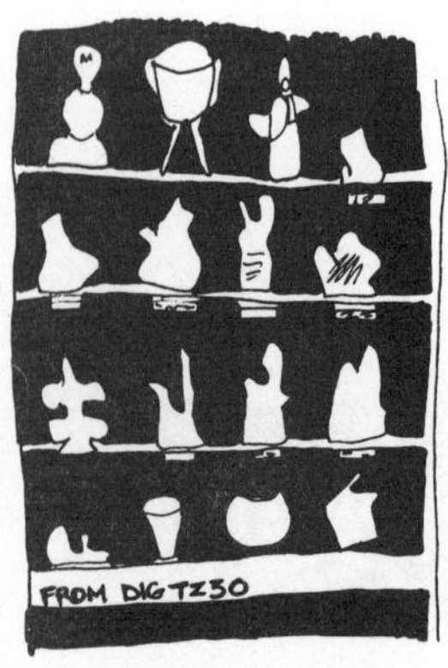

DIG UP THE GROUND

You get dirty hands, blisters and a few pieces of pottery or ancient corroded tools — which doesn't add up to much of a pay-off for hours of back-straining excavating, does it? But look at it this way: *you're uncovering history.*

That's what archaeology is all about. And young people are digging in sites all over the United States, uprooting the past. For example:

- In Pennsylvania, the Westmoreland County Historical Society, along with the University of Pittsburgh, is digging at Hanna's Town. Go there on a sleepy summer afternoon and you will find two or three students working over a small area with spades and trowels. While you watch, perhaps they will unearth bits of clay pots to add to their discovery pile.

You walk around the digs. A house has been reconstructed on traces of foundation uncovered earlier. Other foundations lie piecemeal, etching areas of more buildings. Sign up with the historical society and you can dig, too.

- Throughout Arkansas, amateur archaeologists are unearthing similar sites. Pay a small registration fee at the University of Arkansas Museum, and you can train and dig under professional supervision.

- More digging is available for those of you who live in Illinois near the Koster Site. There, in the river valleys, villages lie one on top of another — going back to the earliest people. Supposedly, they lived in 8,000 B.C. Who were they? How did they live? Those involved in this Northwestern University-sponsored dig hope to find the answers by clawing up America's roots.

If you are close enough to these specific finds, you have fun and challenge first-hand. Otherwise, find out what sites are closer to home. Talk to old-timers who might know. Check with your school or city librarian. Telephone county or state historical societies. Ask at museums. Write to state colleges' and universities' archaeological departments.

You have a whole new world waiting for you — underground.

FOLLOW YOUR GOOD INTENTIONS

Try giving yourself away, as David Dunn advocates in a small book by that name.

Connie does. She gives away compliments, appreciation, kindness, sympathy. And these gifts cost her nothing but concern and interest in other people.

How does this teen-ager go about giving herself away? At first, she made a special effort to do something for someone else whenever she was bored. Now, Connie says, she makes a habit of giving herself away a certain number of times each day. This method makes concern for others a natural part of her daily life.

But how does she know what to give away? Connie plays her hunches. Without thinking what people will say, she follows her good impulses. For instance, she wrote her Uncle Bob, congratulating him when he received a business promotion. She helped her neighbor sand his antique Plymouth to ready it for a new paint job. She inked a big "A" on a placecard for her brother on the day he brought home his first "A" in geography.

After reading the book her grandmother had sent her, she wrote a second thank-you, telling how much she had enjoyed the story. She baked and decorated a cake for a neighbor's 80th anniversary. She told her science teacher that she liked his tie, even though her friends called her "brownie."

She follows through with those good intentions most of us postpone indefinitely for fear someone will misinterpret what we mean.

"Giving yourself away is a fun game," Connie says. "Start with compliments. They are the easiest. But be sincere, whatever you do."

HELP WITH MEALS ON WHEELS

What is "Meals on Wheels"? It's an active volunteer service in many communities throughout the United States. Hot, nutritious meals are delivered six days a week to shut-ins who cannot prepare their own meals. Because these meals are delivered regardless of the recipients' ability to pay, the food is often free and financed locally by churches and civic clubs. And the activity would not be possible except for the volunteers who give regular hours to cooking, packing and delivering these meals.

Where do you come into the picture? Offer to drive one of the volunteers around his or her route for a day. Go into the homes with that person. See who are shut-ins. Say hello. For many of these elderly or handicapped, this visit is their only contact with the outside world each 24 hours. Therefore, you will be a breath of fresh air in their monotonous routine.

If you like the experience, you might want to take over the route one day, to enable the regular driver to have time off. This, of course, depends on local rules. And when weather has made driving hazardous, you could offer foot service where autos are snowbound.

Merely getting acquainted with this tremendous program is worth the effort.

HELP WITH THE WORLD HUNGER PROBLEM

Unless you've seen with your own eyes, it's difficult to imagine the poverty that haunts the hordes of people who choke traffic in Cairo, Port-au-Prince or Calcutta. But it's there, challenging food agencies to feed the starving ones.

And that's where *you* can serve. Find out all you can about world hunger. Do what you can through world food agencies. Raise money to give to them. Alert your family and friends to help, too. You may want to start with the following organizations:

1. **UNICEF — the United Nations Children's Fund helps feed children and adolescents throughout the world.** Its main focus is in underdeveloped nations and devastated areas. For years, American youth and children have collected door-to-door contributions, in place of candy for themselves, on Halloween. Have you?

2. **CROP is the Community Hunger Appeal of Church World Service.** Contributions pay for seeds to plant community gardens, for milk for children in refugee camps and for windmills, wells and other water resources that bring good

crops where none have grown before.

3. **Your own church denomination has its own world hunger concern,** no doubt.

    Other things you can do to alleviate hunger are the following:

4. **Encourage (by talking) a change in our national priorities — from production and sale of armaments to production and distribution of food to hungry nations.** Call in on talk shows whenever the subject is discussed. (Yes, kids *do* this!) Give talks about priorities in speech or English classes, youth groups, scout meetings, 4-H Club meetings.

5. **Be willing to change your own life style to meet the needs of hungry people, both here and abroad.** Don't take what you won't eat — like school cafeteria food that you throw in the garbage. Cut out junk foods that aren't nutritious, anyway. Don't overeat. Try fasting one day a week. Eliminate meat from your diet once a week.

6. **Write representatives and senators whenever important legislation comes up.**

7. **Give money and service to hunger relief programs.** Bike, hike, bowl or fast for CROP. Collect for UNICEF. Give to "One Great Hour of Sharing." Collect and/or package donations for Church World Service.

ORGANIZE A SUMMER NURSERY SCHOOL

Nancy recalled her first field trip. "We can take our nursery children on a similar one," she suggested to Sally. "We watched international freighters being loaded in the South Milwaukee harbor. Mom thought we had boarded the ships because our three-wall mural in the school corridor was so convincing."

The two young women were outlining activities for the one-morning-a-week playschool they were starting. To date, they had enrolled six preschoolers. Quite enough to handle for the two of them this first time, they agreed.

They had helped with two nurseries sponsored at their high school, aced their child-care courses and had received their teacher's approval of their summer venture. Nonetheless, planning was important, they realized. "Be prepared with activities for every minute the children are with you," Ms. Smythe had repeated like a broken record.

So this they did. Some of those worthwhile activities are:

1. **Take a field trip to the beach** to collect shells, feed pelicans and gulls, build sand castles and jump free from the waves, like sandpipers do. This could be the climax of the first month.

2. **The next month, the children could make a mural, like Nancy remembered, with colored chalk on butcher shop wrapping paper.**

3. **Construct talking puppets** by cutting out faces from magazines and pasting them on the ends of popsicle sticks. Have preschoolers talk for their puppets, tell stories and dramatize nursery rhymes and fairy tales.

4. **Have children cut squares and rectangles from scrap cloth, and then place them in shoe boxes that match the materials' designs** — plaid, polka-dot, stripes or plain colors.

5. **Play copycat, with children imitating the teacher's actions and facial expressions:** smiling, scowling, pouting, scaring, hurting. Ask youngsters to tell how they feel while making these faces.

6. **Teach tongue-twisters.**

7. **Instruct children to close their eyes and listen, then open their eyes and tell what sounds they have heard.**

8. **Make bird feeders out of plastic milk bottles.**

9. **Prepare a discovery corner, piled with treasure boxes.** Each child may play with one at a time, returning it to the corner when finished with it. In one box, have all kinds of shells; another, buttons; a third, little automobiles. In others, place doll furniture, or makeup and mirrors or dinosaurs.

10. **Blow bubbles.**

11. **Play store with empty boxes.**

12. **Keep a chest of old clean clothes for dress-up.**

Whether you're male or female, you can also start a kiddie camp. But it's best to involve parents to help you whenever you explore outside your own yard. Once-a-week field trips can be effective projects around which you can build your activities for the yard or garage sessions that precede or follow. Drawing, painting, story-telling or acting can focus on what the children saw, heard, tasted, smelled or felt.

For example, you can visit a farm — see cows milked, pump water from a cistern, feed pigs and gather eggs. Then make a mural, impersonate animals or paint blown-out eggs for an egg tree.

Visits to airports, zoos and bakeries are all child-centered trips with fabulous follow-up prospects.

However, *plan, plan, plan!* Solicit adult drivers. Don't do the driving yourself. Label tots with name and address tags strung around their necks. Have parents sign permission slips. Use a buddy system (two-by-two), with an adult or yourself responsible for no more than four children. Schedule and follow a timetable with adequate rest and food stops. Prepare the children ahead of the field trip. Talk over what they will see and do.

You will be wise to conduct your first summer nursery free of charge — except for materials and travel costs. Grateful parents will give you gratuities, which you will accept gratefully, too. But by not charging, you take yourself off the hook regarding regulations and criticism.

For further aid, talk with nursery and kindergarten teachers, children's librarians and mothers of preschoolers. They will have the latest news in child care and play.

RECYCLE SOMETHING

A Scotsman, renting for a couple of months, came out of his condominium with his arms full of newspapers. "Where do I put these papers?" he asked his teen-aged neighbor.

"In the trash bin."

"What a waste! In Scotland, we would put these in a recycle container."

Your parents would have, too — a few years ago. In fact, your older brothers and sisters probably recycled bottles, paper, aluminum and tin. Recycling was a socially recognized and profitable pastime. Now the activity seems to be outdated. The need for recycling still exists, though.

According to Dennis Hayes, coordinator for Earth Day and Sun Day, two-thirds of material things Americans waste could be reused without changing our life style. Polls indicate that citizens are willing to recycle.

Then why shouldn't you teen-agers recycle the recycle idea? Why not start collecting old metal, for instance? It is precious and will pay you well. Inform your neighbors that you are willing to take such items when they are ready to discard them. Anything from gold inlays to rusty radiators. You have a rich field to mine, since it is estimated that 70 percent of all metal is used only once. Another source for metal is the stream near you, which is reduced to a trickle because rubbish is choking it.

Paper recycling is big business when you make it a group project with deposit bins set where the public can dump.

A Boys' Club in Manatee County (Florida) has three bins — one for newspapers, one for magazines and one for cans. Several churches around the country have paper bins sponsored by Boy Scouts or church youth groups. Door-to-door truck pick-ups on a designated day add to the piles and piles of paper that bring money for group treasuries.

SHOP AT THE SUPERMARKET FOR YOUR PARENTS OR NEIGHBORS

Two husky high-school football tackles strolled up and down the grocery aisles. Their equipment included two calculators, a pad and pencil, a $20 bill, a grocery list and the cart Bill was pushing.

What were these two unlikely characters doing with a graocery cart? Following through a class investigation project, that's what.

With their calculators, they checked the reliability of posted unit prices for canned goods. They figured differences between large and small packaged goods per ounce and per pound, versus package prices of meat. They compared price differences among brands. They noted "good until" dates on cold meats, breads and dairy products. Then using the grocery list, they bought as many items as they could, staying within the $20 limit.

And all the time, they were being watched. Bud described the surveillance in his report: "The clerks looked at us kind of funny-like. Finally, a store manager accosted us. We said we were doing an investigative report for class. That satisfied him, more or less. He kept his eyes on us, though."
The boys moved on to another store the next week. This time, they compared the prices in the two stores. Their final report covered five supermarkets. As a result, the boys consider themselves well-informed consumers.

Bill shops quite regularly for his parents, now that football season is over. He even reads the grocery ads, clips coupons and watches for the specials.

Bud's neighbors are benefiting from his investigation. Now he figures he knows enough about brands and prices to buy groceries for the woman at the end of the block. (She keeps house from a wheelchair.) And just this week, he added another shut-in to his grocery-buying mission.

Such a caring project may appeal to you, too. Who knows until you have tried it?

START A BABY-SITTING CLASS

Christy put a clean Pampers diaper over the wet one when Jeff needed to be diapered.

Todd let Nathan go to the bathroom by himself, behind a closed bathroom door. The child flushed his stuffed monkey down the toilet. The overflow flooded the room.

Both Christy and Todd were baby-sitting for the first time. Neither had had experience with brothers or sisters. They were learning by trial and error.

Because baby-sitting is lucrative for both boys and girls, they grab at the first opportunity to make what they think is easy money, little realizing all that is involved. That's why a baby-sitting class can be a real service to your community. Parents, their children and you teen-agers all profit from it.

1. **Survey interested peers.** Make sure you can guarantee six to 12 members for the class.

2. **Next, line up adult volunteers who are each willing to share their professional know-how for one evening.** Possible contacts are nurses, nursery school and kindergarten teachers, children's librarians, dietitians, pediatricians; rescue squad members and Red Cross first-aid instructors. Approach these specialists by accenting the service they will be giving. Arrange time of classes to fit their professional schedules, but

keep it within students' time schedules, too.

3. **Course content will depend on the experts who will give time to the project.** However, plan to cover as many basics as possible, such as: complete infant care — bathing, feeding, diapering; first aid; some child psychology — what to expect at different ages; basic food preparation; instruction in story-telling and playing children's games.

4. **Once you have your program organized, sign up teen-aged friends for instruction.**

5. **To meet any expenses, work out a sharing plan.** Ask each class member to give one-tenth of the first baby-sitting job's remuneration. Or add up expenses and then divide costs equally among the teen-agers taking the course. You might find an organization that would finance such a class for you. If so, approach the groups' members with the idea before you start. Get a written statement of their subsidy.

TEACH OR TUTOR

While the public panics because "Johnny can't read," let's hope you are a Johnny or Jill who *can*. If so, you may help one of your poorly-reading peers meet the reading requirements for graduation. Or you may enjoy helping a foreign student (or other foreign visitors) to understand our American version of English. In fact, you might even help an adult neighbor to read. The challenges are unlimited.

1. **Start with your classmates.**
Try tutoring in any subject you know best. Use texts and daily assignments. Help the student with homework, but don't do it for him or her.

Often, you can get a peer to understand when the teacher cannot. You use a different word choice or see the problem from a different angle.

2.   Members of the second group — foreign students and visitors — need help with words and phrases.

They need your assistance with idioms. For example, a Norwegian American Foreign Exchange student's host said, "I'll run you over." He was offering to take Erik to the store.

The young man looked puzzled. "Why do you want to run over me?" he asked.

Another time, Erik's American brother said, "It's raining cats and dogs." Erik rushed to the window. What would he see? he wondered.

You can interpret local expressions, too. For example, "soda pop," "pop," "soda," "tonic" and "soft drink" all refer to the same thing. Which term you use depends on where you live. Likewise, "merry-go-round," "flying horses" and "carrousel" are all the same thing. Or people in your region may call a sack a "poke."

3.   The third group you can help are non-reading adults in your area. Contact a local literacy group that adapts the Frank Laubach method of "each one teach one." (This is how he taught millions of people around the world to read and write.)

The usual procedure is for a volunteer to join a class that will instruct him or her in the Laubach method. This is a 12-hour course. You will become familiar with the simple text and be taught how to use it. Then you will be assigned a pupil, with whom you promise to meet twice a week. The books you would use are paperbacks in large type, with picture keys in the margin. When your student completes the five books that make up the course, he or she should be reading at a sixth-grade level.

If you are interested and have no local literacy group, start your own. Get a copy of Dr. Laubach's book, *Each One Teach One*, from your public library. In it are simple drawings and examples of his method, as used in isolated geographic pockets around the world. Once you see these pictures, you will catch his enthusiasm for teaching one person at a time to read and write.

You can also write to chapters of Literacy Advance. (For instance, the National Affiliation for Literacy Advance is active in St. Petersburg, Florida.)

Next, find a pupil. You may want to contact your Visiting Nurses Association for suggestions. Other leads may come from the Parent-Teacher Association, ministers, doctors, lawyers and social workers.

Although illiteracy is a hushed subject in the United States, people who can't read are everywhere. In fact, the number increases with the influx of migrant workers, Haitians and Cubans. Therefore, if you are a good reader, here's your chance to help others learn to read. Why not start right now?

TEACH YOUR SKILL TO SOMEONE ELSE

- Sure, Jill was a paid lifeguard at the high-rise apartment complex pool, but that didn't mean she had to teach residents' grandchildren how to swim. However, this she did after hours and on her days off. Nor did she charge for the instruction, although she could have. "I get paid my salary," Jill explained. "The rest is service to others — in this case, children."

- Before Nancy went to Brazil as a foreign exchange student, Sam offered to teach her Portuguese. He had been born in Mexico and had spent his early years in Rio. Because of his patience and skill with the language, Nancy picked up enough words and phrases to ease the shock of living with a non-English-speaking family.

- Betty Lou loaned her typewriter and manual to Jeff the summer before he entered college. She also checked his assignments. "That's easier than typing your term papers for you," she teased.

- Rick taught two of his buddies how to handle the sound equipment at his church. "I'm helping myself at the same time," he said. "I won't have the whole audiovisual load on my shoulders if I train other guys to give me time off."

- It took the patience of Job, but Tom taught his brother how to bake a cake. "Mom showed me," said Tom. "I figured I'd save her the hassle with Nate."

- And Sally taught four little neighbor kids how to twirl a baton. That was the summer after she had won the state championship, and the children idolized their heroine. The lessons became a nightly show for the whole neighborhood to watch.

- And Ruben taught knot-tying to his mother's den of Cub Scouts.

Are these enough examples to show the variety of skills that can be shared? Now, what is your particular know-how? Someone is eager to learn the skill from you. So share your talents!

TELEPHONE A LONER

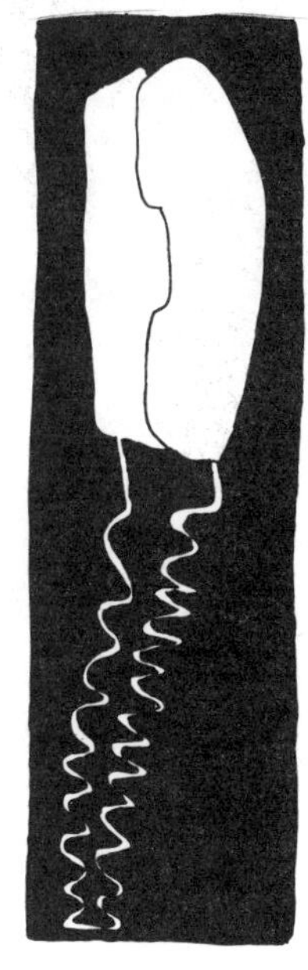

Loners are in your classes. You know, those teen-agers who don't quite jive with the crowd. You can spot them in the school cafeteria, eating alone, or in the hallways, walking alone to and from classes. They are in no social clique, have no boy- or girlfriends. In the classroom, you hardly know they are there.

Your natural reaction is to leave them alone. You figure they prefer their own company. This is not necessarily so. Chances are, they crave friendship. They just lack that outgoing, back-slapping physical display that would ease them into the gang.

1.   Why not speak to one of these outsiders?
Simply say hello and call him or her by name. Ask questions about an assignment — or any other questions you know the loner can answer without embarrassment. Thus, you will help build up his or her confidence and self-esteem.

2. Once you have established the breakthrough, try telephoning. Make the call casual but interesting. Inquire what an assignment is, or suggest joining one of the school clubs to which you belong. Don't push, though. Simply make contact. If the loner wants to talk further, fine. If not, you have shown that you care.

You may gain a new friend. You may even prevent a teen-age suicide by showing your personal concern, if your call coincides with one of those terrifying dips in teen-age emotions. Who knows?

VISIT THE ELDERLY

Two California teen-agers have formed Spring and Autumn Alliance. "Elderly people make fascinating friends," says one of the founders. "Our project brings wisdom to us, enthusiasm to them."

These students visit the elderly in nursing homes, retirement centers and individual residences. They find that talking with people who were married 70 years ago is incredible. And when they ask questions, the older people's memory banks spill forth pioneer stories that top any television drama.

Anna Leah has her own contact with elderly people when she sells her Avon products. She says they are her best customers. She has learned to take her time while with them, listen to their stories and share her own activities with them. "I honestly enjoy talking with old people," Anna Leah admits. "They are living history. And they are so grateful for my visits."

If you have not visited recently with an elderly person, try it. Start with someone in your own neighborhood. It need not be a long visit, or a formal one. Just drop by while the old gentleman is walking around his yard or sitting on his porch. Pass the time of day. Before you know it, you will be caught up in a reminiscing trip that will spark your disbelief. A word of warning, though: expect to listen rather than talk, once you have opened the conversation.

Beth, another teen-ager in Pennsylvania, became so intrigued with her elderly neighbors' life stories that she decided to tape her conversations with them (with their permission, of course). Her finished recordings became historically valuable as local anecdotes and events came to life. Later, she shared the tapes with school, church and community organizations. Here was local color no other person had uncovered.

VISIT VETERANS' HOSPITALS AS CLOWNS

Teen-agers are welcome visitors at veterans' hospitals. You offer vitality, freshness and enthusiasm that patients appreciate. Just your presence, smile, personal greeting and handclasp are therapeutic.

One Key Club has initiated something more: clown therapy. With painted faces and silent antics, these young people have penetrated the depression and withdrawal that these socially isolated soldiers experience. In fact, so successful were these clown ventures in hospitals and nursing homes that Key Clubs all over the United States are being encouraged to organize clown therapy groups. The idea is used by church youth groups, too.

You may enjoy clowning for veterans. Before you and your friends start clowning around, however, here are guidelines passed down by those who have performed:

1. **Contact a veterans' hospital to find out whether or not your services are acceptable.**

2. **Next, try to find a professional clown with whom you can talk.** Ask him or her to show you some techniques. Find out what makes a clown so disarming. When a real clown is not around, read about famous ones and work out your own act.

3. **Collect your costume from rummage sales:** over-sized footwear, balloon-like pants, bright shirts and skirts, crazy hat.

Any rakish combination is high fashion for clowns.

4. **And then create your own clown face.** Happy or sad, it will be a symbol of goodness and fun.

5. **Now you are ready to practice on neighbor kids before you make your first veterans' hospital visit.** It's amazing what you can do behind a clown face. Enjoy yourself!

Enjoy Solo Activites

BRAINSTORM ONE-TIME THINGS TO DO

"What's there to do?" you ask yourself on occasions when you're fed up with your usual routine. You want some action right then and there. Something immediate. Something stimulating.

For answers to that dilemma, brainstorm for ideas to fill that void in the future. Then follow through each activity that makes sense. Repeat those you like.

To stimulate your own brain cells, here are some suggestions, brainstormed in 15 minutes by one person:

1. **List 10 pleasant experiences you have had in the last week.**

2. **Blow bubbles with the neighbor kids, or by yourself.**

3. **Plan ways you can make $100.**

4. **Make a greeting card and send it to a friend.**

5. **Construct a bird feeder from coat hangers and a scrap of plywood.**

6. **Ask your parents about their jobs.** What do they actually *do*? How much do they earn? What are their frustrations?

7. **Write new lyrics to a current top hit.**

8. **Make a check list of places you would like to visit.**

9. **Do prone-position exercises.**

10. **Start a savings account.**

11. **Write to a friend who has moved away.**

12. **Do a good deed.**

13. **Make a scrapbook for a children's hospital.**

14. **Write a "Dear Abby" or a "Dear Ann Landers" letter and send it to the newspaper that carries either column.**

15. **Write a description of your ideal boyfriend or girlfriend.**

16. **List your likes and dislikes.**

17. **Look through magazines and newspapers for recipes of your favorite dishes.**

18. **Collect free brochures on sight-seeing.** Look for them in bus and air terminals, hotels, motels and restaurants.

19. **Draw a detailed map directing friends and relatives to your home.**

20. **Make up a game.**

21. **Tell or read a story to your little brother or sister or neighbor's kid.**

22. **Shoot baskets or play hopscotch with the neighborhood children.**

23. **List your dilemmas.** Concentrate on the most puzzling. Try to solve it.

24. **Note dates on coins in your pocket.**

25. **List surnames you like.** Then check their meanings in dictionaries or other sources.

26. **With your parents' permission, invite a schoolmate to have dinner with you — someone whom you have never before entertained.**

27. **Check food prices in the newspaper advertisements and share bargain facts with your parents.**

28. **Browse through a supermarket hardware department.**

29. **Take a walk through a park, meadow or woods.** See how many trees you can identify — or weeds, shrubs, flowers or bird calls.

30. **Clip out newspaper items about people you know (or don't know) and mail these to them.**

31. **Talk to yourself out loud.** Vocalize your inner speech.

Now carry on from this sampling. Do your own brainstorming. Write down every activity you can think of, however wild. Allow yourself 15 minutes. Remember, these are things you can accomplish in one small parcel of time. Once you have your list, check the plausible ones. Put each on a single slip of paper. Keep these in a box. When you want something to do, draw one of your suggestions from the box and follow through with the act.

Incidentally, you may want to add the above ideas to your box — at least those that fit your interest.

CHANGE YOUR PHYSICAL APPEARANCE

A "new you" is the thrust of most advertisements for beauty aids. And even though these hyperboles disenchant, you can be a quick-change artist. Scissors, diet and different clothes have transformed many a teen-ager into a more likeable self.

It's fun to experiment, and usually not disastrous. If your first hair-coloring experiment doesn't succeed, try another color. (No more green hair after a dive into a chlorinated pool, like big sister experienced.) If your haircut is too short, hair grows, and you can wear a wig in the meantime.

The point is, *you can look almost any way you want* if you dare to be different. Other teen-agers are changing their self-images, and liking it.

- For instance, Kevin went to school with a curly top. It caused much comment because he looked like someone else. However, he put up with the ridicule because he liked his new look.

  "What happpened?" moaned his friend, Ted.

  "Mom gave me a permanent, at my request," explained Kevin. "I like it. So lay off!"

  Ted said no more.

- Fourteen-year-old Leslie was unhappy because too many people mistook her for a boy. She was entering high school and wondered what she could do about her mistaken identity.

  "Wear a dress in place of jeans," suggested a wise senior.

  Leslie did, and skirts provoked a more feminine image.

- Buck was the jolly fat boy, whom everyone enjoyed but Buck himself. He finally made up his mind to lose 50 pounds. By eliminating junk foods and following his doctor's suggested diet, he slimmed down in three months. It took willpower. There was no overnight transformation.

  "It was worth not going to the cafeteria for lunch," Buck said. "I like the new me."

Look in the mirror. What do you see? Is there something about your physical self you can change for the better — or to give you a psychological lift?

CHECK UP ON YOUR HEALTH HABITS

Do you want to live beyond the age of 50? Yes, half a century sounds a long way off to you *now*, and to think of ever being *that* old is appalling. What you do now can't possibly make that much difference, can it? Ah, but it can. Ask your doctor. Ask the nutrition experts. Study heart and lung cancer statistics and you won't be so blasé.

To be scientific about your present life style, get a copy of the *Health Risk Profile*, by Dr. Charles Ross. Take the test. Find out your computer score. Then cut out the evils in your present way of living.

Apparently this test has an uncanny way of pinpointing how your daily habits, as compared with those of others of your age and sex, will lengthen or shorten your life. All this is done on paper, similar to an IQ test. No buttons, no dials, no tubes, such as those required for physical exams. You answer a series of 53 questions, such as:

Do you smoke, drink or drive?
Do you have periods of depression?
Do you eat a wide variety of foods?
Are you overweight?
Do you exercise?

Your score reflects your amount of self-indulgence in categories that cover exercise, nutrition, alcohol and drug use, road and water safety, personal health and general items like television-watching.

The whole idea of the questionnaire is to change human behavior in order to extend life span. Therefore, the sooner you find out how *you* rate, the better the chance you have to live longer, according to Dr. Charles Ross of the University of California.

This human timetable is being used by schools, corporations and health organizations. If you live in southern California, you can get your profile and computer print-out paid for by Blue Cross. Otherwise, see your school nurse for the address to which to write for the questionnaire.

You may save your own life. At least you will change your present life style. Test or no test, take time to evaluate where you are heading physically while still in your teens. You can't change the effects of all that candy you ate as a child. But you can do something about further tooth decay. You can't do anything about the junk food you ate last night. But you can avoid it in the future. And so it goes, ad infinitum.

CLEAN YOUR ROOM

Is your room a cyclonic mess? If so, you have lots of company, for teen-agers are noted for their unkempt rooms.

For example, as a paragraph-writing assignment, sophomores used the following topic sentence: "My teen-aged friend's room was a disaster." Is this a description of your room, too? Then why not bring order to chaos now that you have a little free time?

1. **Throw out everything that is useless.**

2. **Put necessities in their places.**

3. **Hang up clothes.**

4. **Organize your drawers.**

5. **Put your small collectibles in empty shoe boxes.**

6. **Make a map of your room, if you must, to show you where you have put everything.**

7. **Clear off all top surfaces, but leave absolute necessities.** This makes a neat impression, even if your closets' contents are stacked.

8. **Now you are ready to use a scrub brush and vacuum cleaner.**

If you do not fit into this teen-ager syndrome, if you can't stand a crooked shade or one pillow being fuller than its mate, you can still clean your room. Start with the scrub brush and vacuum! None of us is free of honest-to-goodness dirt, unfortunately.

DAYDREAM AND MAKE YOUR DREAMS COME TRUE

"Don't just *sit* there. Get up and *do* something!" When was the last time one of your parents said that to you? Chances are you *were* doing something at that very moment. You were *daydreaming,* weren't you? And according to Dr. Jerome I. Singer, a psychology professor at Yale University, "your capacity to daydream is one of the greatest resources you have as a human being." So don't feel too guilty. Just find a better time and place to do your dreaming.

Supposedly, you spend 30-40 percent of your waking hours daydreaming about almost any imaginable subject. It's the stuff that triggers great ideas, inventions and solutions to problems. Anyone can do it. What you want, though, is to make your dreams work for you. And that takes positive thinking, practice and real-life application.

Use daydreams to rehearse life situations, such as:

- how you will approach Dad when you want the car so you can take your friends to an out-of-town basketball game.
- what you will say when you phone for a date.
- what you will say while serving on that panel about drinking.

Use daydreams to calm your nerves. Before making a free throw, imagine yourself successfully tossing the ball through the hoop. While waiting to give an oral report on your science project, imagine yourself beside a quiet pond with wild ducks lazily drifting through the cattails. In the dentist's chair, recall last night's walk in the moonlight, while the dentist punctures your gums with Novocaine.

If your instant replay or thrusts into new visions are fuzzy, try to sharpen those inner pictures:

1.   Relax.

2.   Let your mind wander.

3.   Focus on a good daydream.

4.   Guide your images to do what you want them to do.

5.   Replay it until you are satisfied.

6.   Then live that dream — expect it to come true!

And next time your parents say, "Don't just sit there. Do something," why not let them know that you *are* doing something. Then share with them some of your dreams.

TRANSPORT YOURSELF
TO THE CONDUCTOR'S STAND

Were you to enter his room unannounced, you would likely see Gary conducting an imaginary orchestra. His musicians are a symphony recording on his stereo, or a live philharmonic orchestra performing on television. And Gary is conducting with all the antics of a professional.

Immediately, you will sense that Gary has innate musicality and a fine sense of rhythm. That's why he's not content simply to sit and listen to these great works. He involves himself in the music he hears. And he does this without any audience.

Try entertaining yourself this way. For whether or not you have Gary's sense of rhythm, you still can add a new dimension to listening by conducting, just as you do by dancing to music in the privacy of your own room. If this activity doesn't come naturally for you, start by observing and aping a conductor as he or she performs on television. Whenever the cameras pick out specific actions, note his or her exact movements and mimic them.

Or you may prefer to tap out the rhythm in music you hear. Either way, you are actively listening.

EXPRESS YOURSELF IN GRAFFITI

Graffiti — picture-writing — covered walls in ancient Rome and Pompeii. Today these scratchings blemish buildings, telephone booths, stop signs — wherever people can scrawl without being caught.

Graffito is a form of self-expression. When teen-agers are suppressed or too harshly disciplined, for instance, they chip their defiance into school desks or restroom walls. Some graffiti express political points of view. Other slogans and signs state social demands. Even religious statements appear. Still other words and initials are cries for self-recognition. "Notice me!" they are saying.

Haven't you ever carved your initials in a tree trunk? Or scrawled initials, phrases and pictures with a felt pen on a school desk? Or chalked the sidewalk?

There's something about human nature, it seems, that creates strange ways of self-expression. And graffito is one. So why not put this vehicle of self-expression to work for you where it does not destroy?

1. **Find yourself a spot that is secret, away from the eyes of others.** Your bedroom closet wall will do, or even the inside of your closet door.

2. **Paint the surface white or a pastel color.**

3. **Scribble with washable crayons, such as preschoolers use.**

4. **Any time you feel angry, ugly or hateful, express your feelings on this graffiti board.** Don't erase until you

are through exploding in symbols and pictures.

Later, when your frustrations have eased, look at your graffiti. Try to understand what provoked you. Then calmly try to find constructive ways of dealing with whatever or whoever upset you.

5. **You may also use your graffiti board for visual thinking or dreaming.** Use it, for instance, when you're in love — or think you are. Write that boy or girl's name or initials. Draw hearts and flowers and smiles, or whatever you think identifies that person.

Or identify yourself. Write, "Who am I?" Then answer the question in symbols, words and pictures. Do you see the possibilities?

GET ACQUAINTED WITH YOURSELF

How well do you know your body, mind and spirit? Read. Question. Find answers to what you don't know.

1. **First, discover the intricacy, efficiency and power of that miraculous body of yours.**

You probably have some understanding if you have had classes in biology and chemistry. For instance, did you learn that:

- More than half of the 206 bones in your body are in your hands and feet?

- If the 600 muscles in your body all pulled in the same direction, you could lift 25 tons?

- Your heart pumps five-six quarts of blood a minute, but when you run it will pump up to 40 quarts a minute, if necessary to meet muscle demand?

- Your ear can distinguish more than 300,000 tones?

Ask your school librarians or science teachers to recommend books and visual aids that will answer your questions about the human body.

Watch public television programs about the care and feeding of the human body. Treat your own body as a precious, sacred gift. Eat nutritious foods. Avoid physical habits that tear down the body. Exercise in moderation.

2. **Find out about your mind next.** Seek answers to questions like the following:

- How do you think?
- How and where do you store memories?
- What causes you to create?
- How do you learn?

Again, your information sources are in libraries, both public and school. Explore the psychology book sections. Look under "mind" and "brain" in the *Reader's Guide to Periodical Literature* for current listings of magazine articles.

Ask questions of experts in the field, whenever you have the opportunity.

Buy or borrow a book on how to improve your memory and practice the exercises it offers.

3. **Tune in to your inner feelings** — your conscience, spirit, soul — whatever you want to call that intangible quality that makes you the very special person you are.

To know yourself better spiritually, don't be afraid to ask yourself questions, whether or not you can answer them at this time in your life.

Here, for example, are some starters called "thoughts about me:"

Who am I?

A bit of atomic dust?
A child of God?
A piece of eternity?

A member of society?
A unique form of life?
A person dependent on my peers?

But how do I know who I really am?

Do I have faith in myself? In what I can do?
Do I have faith — trust — that God is part of me? That I am part of His great plan?
Do I have a personal code or philosophy? Can I live with it?
Are peers and friends more important to me than morals?
Can I be trusted?
Can I live with myself?
Can I relate to the total universe?
Do I have faith in the importance of life? Faith that life has purpose and meaning?
Is my concept of myself a growing one?
Do experiences and exposures to others help me adapt?
Am I lonely sometimes?
Do I love myself?
Do I love my neighbor as myself?
Am I lovable?
Do I put first things first?
Do I keep faith in the face of pressures?

KEEP A HAPPINESS BOOK

Bonnie reports that each night, she tries to recall one happy event of the day, think about it and record it. "In this way, I go to sleep happy and wake up happy," she says.

The entries on her pages include:

Happiness is sand squeaking under your feet on the beach.
Happiness is finding out that you are not as dumb as you think you are.

> Happiness is having the right answer when the teacher calls on you.
> Happiness is taking a hot bath after you have been soaked in a downpour at a football game.
> Happiness is your little brother telling you a secret.

To you, happiness may be a number of very personal things that you accept every day. But if you go on a happiness binge like Bonnie's, you will find new appreciation for the everyday activities that otherwise pass unnoticed.

For instance, happiness may be a long-distance telephone call, a new book, a ride in a Porsche, a cotton-candy sky or beach-combing after a storm. Happiness may be an animated conversation, a smile or a word of encouragement. Happiness may be smelling a freshly-baked pizza and knowing you can eat all you want of it. Happiness may be lips brushed across your cheek.

Happiness was some particular experience or feeling *you* had today. Have you thought about it? Recorded it?

Not only does keeping a happiness book call for action, but it also boosts your morale. Instead of concentrating on your peeves, hurts, humiliations and dislikes, you are accenting the positive.

Happiness can be keeping a happiness book!

KEEP A JOURNAL

Writing in a journal can be an emotional outlet. Within its pages, you can vent your feelings without injuring anyone and can think creatively in the process. For example:

1. **Explode your temper in written put-downs in place of spoken nasties.**

2. **Practice writing love letters.**

3. **Record conversations you would like to have with that fellow or girl who turns you on.**

4. **Pen your moods** — indigo blue or jealous green, flaming red or bright yellow.

5. **Explore your feelings toward parents, siblings, friends and teachers.**

6. **List your likes and dislikes.**

7. **Examine your pet peeves.**

8. **Work off your resentments and hostilities.**

9. **Describe people you admire and would like to emulate.**

10. **Discuss global events and how they affect you.**

11. **Give opinions and pinpoint why you have them.**

12. **Take a stand on an issue; defend it with evidence.**

13. **Expose your fears and hang-ups.**

    You may write anything in a journal. Cover as many pages as you need, whenever you feel like it — tonight, next year or when you're 21. It's a take-it-or-leave-it enterprise. No continuity. No five-lines-a-day. All you need is a ledger-sized notebook with blank pages.

MEDITATE

Meditation is like a revolving stage. It accommodates many scenes. You can meditate while lying on a sun deck beside a swimming pool. You can stand on your head in a corner, Yoga-style. You can sit in a cathedral and watch sunbeams dance through stained glass windows. You can sit on a stump in a snow-bedecked forest, deer rifle in hand.

To meditate means different things to different people. Therefore, you have several choices of aids to use in "thinking deeply and continuously."

1. **Some Eastern religious groups, for instance, base much of their success on selling the "nothingness" depth of meditation.** Relax. Rid yourself of all thought, feeling and activity.

2. **Our Western practices of meditation limit that mind purge.** They accentuate the positive. You, the participant, are asked to wipe out all thoughts of pain, tension, hatred — those things which destroy happy living.

    You then fill your mind with creative, inspiring, beautiful thoughts. Prayer is often so patterned. Singers and speakers practice this type of relaxation.

    Northwestern University School of Speech students, for instance, use a meditation exercise to relax the throat muscles and help produce richer vocal tones. During private instruction, the performer sits in a fan-backed chair, with eyes closed. The instructor then asks the student to relax by recalling a serene setting (a calm inland lake, perhaps, with the silence broken only by bird calls). The student orally describes the scene in a droning, half-hypnotic voice.

3. **Psychics who sell mind power for profit offer similar meditation exercises.**

    One source, for example, suggests you sit upright in a straight chair. Close your eyes. Think of a lovely flower garden. Concentrate on a single flower in that garden. Note a dewdrop on the velvet petal. See how it glistens. Now move away from that flower a few feet. Lie down on the grass and dream about anything you wish, like a mailbox full of mail.

    The exercise includes several other steps. But note that the same process of relaxation, concentration and filling your mind with a single desire is, in the end, supposed to give you the mind power to will the appearance of that money, job or friend or whatever.

Through the metaphysical meditation just described, you supposedly make contact with the life energy of the universe. You put up an antenna, so to speak, to receive that encompassing power. You tune in. Once you feel you are part of this larger energy resource, you are charged with abundant enthusiasm, drive and direction. A type of self-hypnosis? Perhaps. A religious pattern? Maybe.

Evangelists often follow a meditation plan. Ruth Carter Stapleton, sister of former President Jimmy Carter, is an example of one who did. She played her audience like an organ, willing them to shut their eyes and listen while she directed their thoughts. She sent them back to early childhood to see their fathers and mothers. She had them try to understand *why* their parents had acted the way they did, *why* there were misunderstandings, hurts and heartaches. By acknowledging these hurts, she *willed* changed attitudes and relationships.

Yes, meditation has many outlets. It can be a very personal experience enacted in your own room. It can be group involvement. You can be silent. You can talk to yourself. You can follow directions given by another person, trying to tune you in to other wavelengths.

Whatever process you follow, you will gain another dimension to living, say teen-agers who practice meditating. So don't pooh-pooh the idea until you have at least given it a try.

START RUNNING

Not so long ago, LSD meant a drug trip. Today, for a whole new breed of health-conscious runners, it stands for a **l**ong, **s**low **d**istance run.

Runners get high — a natural high, they will tell you. Ask that buddy who runs three miles on a country road before going to school. He feels exhilarated and buoyant, he insists. And if you pump him further, he likely will extol running as a sport, exercise and hobby. Also, he will point out that it is almost free: "All you need are the right shoes and determination."

If such enthusiasm persuades you to join him (and the thousands of teen-agers running all over the country), here are guidelines to help you. They are but a sampling of hundreds of helpful hints offered in running books, magazines and newsletters.

1. **Don't scrimp on running shoes.** They are your shock absorbers.

2. **Don't expect quick results.** If you try to do too much too fast, you'll pull muscles or be too tired, and feel miserable.

3. **If running hurts, stop.** Try something else.

4. **As long as you cover 1½ miles four or five times a week, at a moderate pace, you'll stay in shape.**

5. **Increase your running mileage gradually.**

6. **Occasionally run with a friend.** Time will pass more quickly. And the companionship will take your mind off minor discomforts.

7. **Run different courses for variety.**

8. **Make running a lifelong sport.**

9. **Running is an aerobic routine that speeds up heart and breathing rates.** When carried on for an hour at least three times a week, it may keep the blues away and uplift you mentally.

10. **It's supposed to be fun. Enjoy!** Compete only if you are on the track team or in the Boston Marathon.

SEND FOR A LIVING WILL

"What if I were kept alive by artificial means when I could never again be more than a living vegetable?" The thought haunts you. You have just been discussing mercy-killing (euthanasia) with your peers. And you know from the way they attack it that the question is a big one. It's filled with emotional overtones and religious implications. Nonetheless, you understand the realities of euthanasia. You saw your grandfather suffer through months of a terminal disease.

But what can you do about the problem, personally? Write for a copy of "The Living Will." The address is:

The Euthanasia Educational Council
250 W. 57th Street
New York, New York 10019

There is a small fee. After it arrives, discuss its meaning with friends and family.

What is a "living will?" Briefly, it states that under certain conditions, you have a right to die. If the time comes when there is no reasonable expectation of your recovery, you request that you be allowed to die, and not be kept alive through artificial means. More than 3,000,000 copies have been distributed.

A copy will give you ammunition for further debates on mercy-killing. And it may turn out to be something you want for yourself, if you believe you have a right to die with dignity.

SHOO THE BLUES AWAY

Teen years are exciting, full of action and promise, but they're confusing, too. And depressing at times, because of pressures and not being able to get your own way.

Along comes a day — or even a whole week — when nothing seems to go right. Three kids jump the cafeteria line ahead of you. In French class, you flunk a pop quiz. Your steady dropped you for your best friend. Could anything be worse?

You start yelling at your mom. You kick the cat out of your way. You're even ready to throw stones at the vacant house across the street. But wait a minute! Before you go berserk, try a few self-administered remedies, guaranteed to change your indigo blue mood to a brighter one (at least so say those who have tried them).

Here they are — bold and crazy — but usually therapeutic:

1. **Shout your anger to the wind or waves.** This is easy to do if you live near a woods or seashore away from people.

2. **Otherwise, jog around the block once, twice, three times — as many times as it takes to crucify your anger.** "I feel wonderful," said Jan, "after jogging to the circle twice and taking a shower."

3. **Or, as Dr. Lois Miller, clinical psychologist, advised over the radio, "Go to your room. Lock the door. And pound a pillow until the feathers fly. Better yet, get yourself a punching bag."**

   If you have a room to cry in, you may want to try one or all of these less violent activities to let off steam before the lid blows off:

4. **Grab some old newspapers. And while you play your stereo, tear the paper into shapes that you see in your mind's eye as your hear classical or rock music or whatever you feel like playing.**

   Repeat your performance. Compare your paper shapes. What do you think they tell you about yourself?

5. **On typewriter-sized paper, draw a vertical line down the middle.** Head the left side, "likes;" the right, "dislikes." Try to list twice as many of your likes as you do your dislikes.

6. **Grab a piece of rope or heavy cord, about 18 inches long.** Tie a knot in it for each person you can think of who has influenced your life *positively*. If you stay with this activity long enough, the rope will become a huge ball.

7. **On any scrap of paper, try writing a poem, prayer or song.** Some of the world's most inspiring selections were written in moments of despair and frustrations — such as those by Edgar Allan Poe and Lord Byron.

Debby worked off her frustrations and hurts in free verse when she broke up with her boyfriend. It was lyrical beauty that she never did duplicate during happy times. "It was an emotional release," she explained.

Tar-pit plunges seem to be part of the process of growing up. Not that such a fact is any consolation. But with every dip of your emotional roller-coaster, there's a high in the future. And these activities aim to help you look up and love life once more.

A word of warning, though: these are just bandages for the bruises and cuts of teen-agers' feelings — the everyday knocks. If depression persists, see your doctor, school counselor or minister. They *want* to help you.

TAPE YOURSELF

For a personal pastime, get acquainted with your speaking or singing voice. With a tape recorder turned on, you can:

1. **Read a mystery story aloud, tell a joke or quote poems or read your favorites.**

2. **Verbalize your inner speech** — those conversations you carry on continually within yourself — dialogues with that fellow or girl you would like to know, for example.

3. **Voice your philosophy.** Tell what you believe.

4. **Conduct an interview with a prospective employer, talking both parts.**

5. **Air your gripes.** Formulate your opinion on a world-shocking problem.

6. **Practice the foreign language you are studying.**

7. **Pretend you are a disc jockey.** Select records to play; work out transitional chatter for fill-in between albums; coordinate a 15-minute program.

8. **Sing your favorite camp or pep rally songs.**

The possibilities for self-entertainment with a tape recorder are endless. And in play-back, you literally get acquainted with your own voice and thoughts. You become objective, once they are on tape.

VISIT YOUR GRANDMOTHER

A Jacksonville, Florida, student gave this advice during a newspaper interview: "Visit your grandmother *today* and have a long talk with her. Don't do it to make her happy. *Do it for yourself.* Once she is gone, most of the information she could have given you about your family history will be buried with her."

This suggestion also goes for *any* grandparents — especially great- and great-great-. No doubt you have wondered about your ancient ancestors, but to think of your grandparents as the closest surviving link to your family lineage is rather shocking, isn't it? There's an urgency to get facts and legends directly. Tomorrow may be too late.

Therefore, visit your grandmother (or great-grandmother, if she is still living) for the sole purpose of digging for your "roots."

Ask a few questions, if necessary, to prime her memory. Otherwise, sit back and let her reminisce. (Later, you can write down facts, names and statistics you wish to remember.) Try not to be impatient. Let the story unfold naturally. Occasionally, you may have to prod her for relationships; she will assume you know, when you don't.

At any rate, keep Grandma remembering. You will be glad you did in years to come.

WRITE ON AN IMPROMPTU BASIS

Remember those fantastic ideas that struck like lightning in your brain? Of course you don't. You never recorded them. At the time, you thought you had the plot of a million-dollar novel. Or was it a whodunit?

Save those fantasies for that best-seller. And sharpen your real-life observations with the same purpose in mind. It's simple: keep a small notebook in your pocket or purse and jot down what you see or feel. When you are bored with waiting for doctor, date or bus, whip it out and write.

Describe a person waiting near you. Note the droop of the shoulders, the sagging mouth, the moth-eaten, faded sweater of the derelict tottering toward the lamp post. Describe how that little boy must feel as he takes his father's hand to cross the six-lane highway. Or write down your own feeling of frustration at being kept waiting.

Whatever you write about, be specific. Roll out the adjectives. Let your imagination flow through your environment. Don't worry about what people will think. At best, they will dub you a reporter. At worst, they may call you daffy. Who cares?

On-the-spot note-taking gives you ammunition for paragraph-writing, composition-writing or creative writing in class; speech-writing; or cutline-writing for cartoons.

> • Harriet even won an essay contest by using scraps of street conversations and descriptions that she had written while waiting for a tardy bus.

● Holed up with his family behind shuttered windows, with only a flashlight to break the blackness, Drew wrote. He described how he felt while hurricane-pressured winds shoved against the house. That real terror turned into his first sale.

WRITE DOWN YOUR LIFE PHILOSOPHY

This isn't the easiest thing to do at this time in your life. It takes much self-searching. Also, your goals are probably not too definite. But grope around. Once you have a sense of purpose, life becomes less hectic. It's like an archer trying to hit the bullseye with an arrow. At least there's exhilaration and challenge in trying.

To help you get started, here are samples of how other teen-agers have spelled out their aims:

● **Larry:** "My goal in life is to become a man whom people respect, and to do work which benefits mankind."

● **Bill:** "My aim in life is to get away from it all. I mean that I don't want to be in a groove. I want to be somebody and still do something different."

● **David:** "My philosophy is that nothing is impossible. I aim to set my goals high. If a person *really* wants something in life, there's *nothing*, from my point of view, that can prevent him or her from getting it."

● **Ralph:** "To take it step by step, day by day, is my philosophy. Many people ruin most of their days worrying about tomorrow. I feel that if you are going to worry, worry about today. Better yet, why worry?"

You see, they don't have all the answers, but these fellows are thinking about what they believe. Have you vocalized or written down your philosophy?

Go Where the Action Is

ATTEND AUCTIONS

Auctions are exciting, whether or not you bid. The crowd thrills with tension as the auctioneer urges bidding higher and higher. You catch the mood.

You have your choice of several types of auctions. They are free. And you need not bid unless you wish.

1. **Currently, motels house one-night auctions of oriental rugs, antiques or used furniture.** The auction company moves in a van full of merchandise. Transient motel guests drift in to watch the excitement. Townspeople who have seen preliminary advertisements show and bid, or just come to watch. You, too, are welcome. Look and listen. Learn the lingo — the auctioneer's babble. Note signals used by bidders. Wise up to planted bidders that raise the ante.

2. **Jewelry auctions are popular in resort areas.** The house policy usually discourages any bidding by a first-time visitor. Attendants allow you to handle diamonds, emerald-set rings and bracelets worth thousands of dollars. However, you will probably feel more comfortable in this setting if you have an adult escort.

3. **Estate settlement auctions are most popular.** Advertisements appear in newspaper classified ad sections. Auctioned off are farm equipment and stock, household goods and antiques.

Try bidding at one of these events, as many pieces go for a dollar or two. Old picture frames, tools, souvenir spoons, old coins, books, dishes, toys — the list of bidding items is endless. Browse first, though. Decide what you might want to bid on and how high you will go. Later, when you do bid, beware of the slick bidder who teases you beyond that cut-off point.

If you can keep your head while bidding, you will have an exhilarating day. If you can't, then stay silent and watch the action.

ATTEND DIFFERENT CHURCHES

You don't have to be a "Jesus freak" to attend various churches. So don't get turned off by the idea without giving it a try — that is, those of you who aren't church-oriented. You have a world of excitement to experience, without getting any more involved than you wish.

The same goes for you who do attend church, who are loyal to one denomination, for instance. You still have other faiths to explore. And by selecting hours or dates that vary from those of your own church's services, you can be both loyal and investigative.

1. **In either case, attach yourself to a teen-ager from another religious denomination or faith.** Ask to accompany him or her to a church service. Explain that you are interested in observing and learning about that particular religion.

   However make it clear from the start that you do *not* wish to be pressured into conversion or membership. Get as many hints as possible ahead of time on how to dress, when to kneel and what the service will be like. During the service, observe and follow procedures and rituals as your friend does. If it's too confusing, though, sit back and watch. Don't panic. Or take part only when you want to or when you feel right about doing it.

   After the service, quiz your friend concerning acts and symbols you did not understand. Since all churches welcome visitors, you can go by yourself. A friend explaining what is happening and why, though, puts you at ease in a strange setting.

2. **Visit traditional Christian denominations,** such as Presbyterian, United Methodist, Lutheran, Episcopal, Baptist, Catholic or Congregational-Christian. Also, visit smaller sects and fringe groups.

3. **And when you have other faiths — Judaism, Hinduism, Islam, etc. — nearby, at least visit their worship sites,** whether or not you worship with them. Most of these have guided tours of their places of worship. Trained personnel will answer your questions.

4. **Also, most of these churches you visit will have active youth groups whose members will welcome a visit from you.** Attend these meetings, too, at their designated times. You will find friendship, concern and commitment over and beyond that of other non-religious peer groups.

    At the end of your church-hopping, you'll probably be the best-informed teen-ager in your community when it comes to what's going on behind all those stained glass windows.

ATTEND A CIRCUS

Circuses aren't what they used to be. The animal-smelly, sawdusty romance of the big top faded away years ago. But who cares? The circus today is an electronically excited extravaganza that surpasses Disney World. Instead of crowding into a sizzling hot tent, you sit in an air-conditioned city arena.

In no way are you cheated. A circus is still a circus, with sawdust and sequins, roaring lions and trumpeting elephants, dancing horses and roller-skating bears and trapeze artists and laughing clowns.

So don't miss the circus if you want two hours of thrills!

ATTEND FOLK FAIRS

Fairs are always fun. But the latest to catch the fancy of teen-agers is the medieval fair. And judging by the crowds that attend them, they are growing in popularity.

New College co-sponsors a medieval fair in March with the Ringling Museum. Students dressed as knights and ladies roam the grounds. Merchants of victuals and spirits offer pastries, cheese, wine, shish kebab and baklava. Sheep-to-shawl demonstrations show shearing, spinning, weaving and dyeing.

Guild members ply their trades: brass-rubbing, hammock-making and glass-staining. One guild even sells "pious frauds, indulgences and costume accessories."

Entertainment at the New College-Ringling Museum event includes grand marches in costume, Punch and Judy shows, a human chess game, archery, medieval magic and productions of "A Doctor In Spite of Himself." Crowds crush around performers. Children climb banyan trees to see. Mounted knights direct traffic. Lords and ladies mingle among the crowd. You easily sense the medieval atmosphere.

Larger cities annually turn their civic arenas into international or folk fairs. Milwaukee and Pittsburgh feature such events. Ethnic groups have food booths. Handicrafts and costumes are for sale. Each country's music and folk dances are part of the entertainment.

If you belong to an ethnic organization, you may have already participated in these gala fairs. However, these glimpses of other cultures are open to the public, luckily. They offer authentic tastes, smells, colors and motions. So check with friends of foreign heritage for the times and place of the next fair in your area.

ATTEND A GARAGE SALE

Second-time-around sales have many names and are held in various locations.

- Garage sales are in garages or carports.
- Flea markets take over parking lots or old barns.
- Rummage sales are held in churches and vacant stores, and occasionally, a big one is held in a municipal arena.
- "Barely-Blemished Sale," "Pampered, Preowned Apparel Sale" and "Daisies-Won't-Tell Sale" are just fancy names for charity fund-raisers, held in large civic buildings.

Regardless of name, these sales all sell junk. But it's valuable, though, to the person who needs that particular item. And sometimes you find a real steal. That's why these sales are so popular.

1. **Attend a garage sale (by whatever name) without any real purpose in mind except to look.** This costs you nothing. Enjoy watching others buy.

2. **Or take with you a restricted cash sum — say $5 — with the idea that you will spend it only if you find something really right for you.**

3. **A third way to approach one of these sales is to search for a definite item, such as** board games, a lamp for your room, records of oldies, hockey skates, something to wear or costume jewelry. Garage sale-hopping can be a fun pastime, if you don't overdo it. You meet all kinds of people. You go into new or different neighborhoods. And sometimes you get a rare bargain.

   So find yourself a sale or two or three. Look in the classified ad section of your newspaper for locations of current sales. Or cruise around until you find a hand-drawn sign saying "garage sale."

ATTEND HOCKEY GAMES

Ice hockey mates violence with beauty: rocket-fast pucks and slashing sticks with gleaming skates and mirror-smooth ice. If you want action and adrenalin-producing excitement, here it is.

1. **You may be lucky enough to have a high-school team to cheer on to victory.** Public school teams are fighting for recognition by the official athletic associations. It is only a short time, though, before this sport will be a major one, say the hockey enthusiasts.

   In the meantime, high-school teams are recruiting outsiders for coaches and officials, paying their own expenses and soliciting student support.

2. **If you live in or near a large city, attend one of the professional games.** These teams hold special youth nights with reduced gate fees, and give away shirts, hockey sticks and pucks. Take advantage of these special nights.

3. **Or watch professional games on television.** The announcers are as emotionally charged as the players.

   To really enjoy the game, however, you should know the basic rules and what the game is all about. Get a player to explain terms: "assist," "back-checking," "boarding," "corners," "face-off," "fore-checking," "freezing," "puck," "penalty-killers," "poke-check," "slapshot," "wrist-shot," etc.

   The object of the game is to put the puck inside the other team's goal and to keep it out of your goal. The game is played on an ice surface, officially 200' x 65'. Lines divide the rink into three zones: offensive, neutral and defensive. A goal is at each end of the ice.

   Take it from there and shout with the crowd.

ATTEND MOTORCYCLE RACES

Either big-time or small-time, motorcycle racing is exciting to watch and much more exciting to compete in, according to one teen-aged rider.

Barney, a 4'10" chubby boy who was often the brunt of jokes, set his classmates right when he told them about his racing in district competition and being sponsored by an accessories firm. He showed the pads, boots, helmet, visor and mouthguard he wears while racing. But the class had difficulty taking him seriously. Little Barney, a sponsored cyclist?

"None of these guys who ride is really big," Barney tried to explain. "How much weight do you want to haul with a 15-cubic-inch engine?"

The next day he brought in his prizes. The class was finally impressed. "My sponsor pays for all my gear. The motorcycle is really theirs, but I get the use of it. I like to race. It makes me feel important. Big."

A few weeks later, the big-timers raced in the civic stadium. Barney was there watching, along with several classmates who had caught his enthusiasm. Professional racers were riding for Yahama and Kawasaki. "That's top class," Barney said. "Factory ride, they call it. See that kid down there? He's just turned 17 and already has a contract with Yamaha, only he has to finish high school — the contract says so."

Barney and his colleagues watched the eight-race card called Supercross. The roar was terrific. The antics, unbelievable.

The next night, Barney and his friends came again, this time especially to watch a pretty 18-year-old woman compete along with 1,300 amateur motorcrossers. "She's the American Motorcyclist Association's women's national amateur champion in her division," Barney said. It took the rest of the night for Barney to explain the point system and standings.

Similar competition takes place wherever cities are willing to build backwoods-style trails for motorcyclists through the middle of their civic stadiums. If you are within reach of these professional races, you can watch top billings. Minus that opportunity, head for the country trails where the Barneys will provide the action, speed, dust and noise that thrill spectators.

ATTEND OLD CAR EXHIBITS

While touring the turnpikes of America, did you ever pass a parade of antique cars? Their occupants probably looked like 1890 ancestors in their old-fashioned clothes. You laughed, no doubt, as you whizzed by. Old pokeys, they were.

In the meantime, you may have met someone in your own town who is fixing up an old model and hanging on to it until it becomes an antique. If you talk with him or her, you will learn how valuable antiques are.

Visiting old car exhibits where showpieces have prices attached will add to your appreciation, too. Malls periodically have such exhibits. Throughout the country, you will find spectacular exhibits to please the public.

One of the finest, and the most complete, permanent exhibits is in Sarasota, Florida, on U.S. 41. Silver Springs, outside Ocala, Florida, also has a commendable display. Stern's Motor Museum, just off the Pennsylvania turnpike in Irwin, is smaller, but exceptional.

In any permanent exhibit, you will see such classics as a 1931 LaSalle V-8, with a small left-side hatch for golf clubs; a 1915 Pierce Arrow Suburban limousine, with domed roof and headlamps inserted in the fenders; or a 1939 V-16 Imperial seven-passenger Cadillac.

These remnants of the past tell their own stories.

ATTEND A SEMINAR

Don't let the word scare you, even though it does remind you of school. It literally means "a group of students getting together to do research." But in the popular adaptation today, seminars are well-attended meetings where a specialist offers a crash course in speed-reading, real estate or making $1,000,000. The specialist has done the research. You simply listen and absorb his or her know-how. And there's something in it for you — *free*.

Look for large ads in your local paper alerting the public to these free seminars. They are one-night stands to hook prospects for courses costing $300-$500 on follow-up weekends. But the initial sales pitch is free and very informative.

You get piles of free literature. You expose yourself to new terminology and new facts. You hear a persuasive introduction to a field you probably know little about.

These seminars are held in motels, hotels or mall meeting rooms. Just walk in. Take a seat. Listen.

Less pressurized seminars are also available to you teen-agers. The YMCA, YWCA, modeling schools and department stores conduct self-help courses on such subjects as improving your appearance, getting jobs in industry and styling hair. These are mini-courses. Some are free. Others ask a small tuition — enough to keep you serious about staying in the program.

Community junior colleges have public seminars that you might like to visit when the subject appeals to you. Sometimes they are open sessions of regular classes with a guest speaker, town meeting or open forum. Others are part of the continuing education program for the county or city. They import specialists on various subjects, from doctors to gardeners, golfers to explorers.

Each session is complete, unattached in subject or personnel to the next one. You pay no tuition. You may attend a single session or the whole series.

Your public library is another seminar source. People in the community, who are experts in their fields, share their experiences. Discussions follow the movies shown.

If you want to expand your know-how, you have all these opportunities beckoning to you. Venture forth! You aren't trespassing in any of these places.

ATTEND SYMPHONY CONCERTS

Expose yourself to another musical dimension by attending a symphony concert at least once. It won't be completely foreign to you, for even if you have had no formal introduction to Tchaikovsky, Dvořák or Verdi, you will recognize familiar tunes among the concertos and arias.

You need not be able to identify what you hear in order to appreciate symphony concerts. Just let your emotional response lead you where it will. You will soon be caught up and carried along with the crescendos and the brilliance of many instruments creating a harmonious togetherness.

For added interest, concentrate on one section of the orchestra, such as the cellos. Or focus on the podium choreography (conductor's antics).

By all means, attend a live symphony concert for the full impact. As second best, however, listen to the fine taped or live presentations on public television.

The Boston Symphony Orchestra's television performances have been popular for years. "Live from Lincoln Center" features symphonies. Other city symphony orchestras are taped during a live performance and presented once or twice during the following week for television viewing.

Tune in for a change from rock or country music. And if you like what you hear, expose yourself to more. Read the concert reviews in the newspapers. Learn the names of famous conductors, like André Previn. Buy student season tickets. Usher at symphony concerts, so that you can listen for free.

GO BACKPACKING

"Backpacking is hiking, plus carrying your equipment and camping out," Wally explained to two friends as he packed for a three-day trip. At 16, he had backpacked for two years. No longer a novice, he figured. But he wasn't ready to tackle Mt. Everest.

"What does backpacking offer that jogging doesn't?" asked Rick, who jogs five miles a day.

"That's like comparing a bicycle with a motorcycle," Wally replied.

"Hey, get with it. Jogging can be rugged. It tests every muscle in your body."

"Right. But backpacking is something more. It takes you away from civilized comforts. It's like pioneering. You get the feel of the primeval. You hear the roar of the waterfalls, smell the cedar logs. You cling to jagged rocks that pierce your hands. There's exhilaration — a high, you might say. And complete exhaustion."

"So? I get exhausted jogging," Rick persisted. "And all those other things, I can have if I jog in the country."

"But you don't camp out — or get lost. Once I was lost for a whole day. I was scared. But when I finally found my way out of that canyon, I felt like I had won an Olympic medal, or something."

"Tell us about your gear," Rick said. "These boots aren't very heavy."

"They shouldn't be big and heavy. That just adds more weight to your feet. They are American-made. The European ones squeeze my toes — too narrow. Also, these are made without seams, except at the heels."

"And your pack?"

"Very light. It's waterproof nylon and has a tubular frame."

John, who had been looking over the piles of equipment during this conversation, asked, "Will you carry all this stuff on your back?"

"Sure. Tent, sleeping bag and pad, cooking utensils, stove, dehydrated food, clothing, raincoat and more."

"Wow! This stuff must weigh a ton: flashlight, insect repellent, snake-bite kit, swimming suit, guidebook, camera, wool sweater. You can't possibly take all that!" John exclaimed.

"Well, I *am* limited by what the pack will hold. Even then, if it weighs more than one-fourth my own body weight, I have to discard and then repack. You learn fast what are essentials."

That's how Wally's two friends learned a bit about backpacking. And had they been interested, he would have advised them further.

You may be as lucky as Wally's friends, if you know a seasoned backpacker. If not, literature abounds to tell you about it.

Backpacker is a magazine full of information on skills, equipment and places to go (Ziff Davis, 1 Park Ave., New York, New York 10016). Among many books devoted to this sport is *Backpacking in the United States*, by Eric Meves (MacMillan Publishing Co., Inc., New York, New York).

GO CAMPING

"You haven't lived until you've been to camp!" Tom exclaimed when he returned from a sailing camp. You will probably agree with Tom's enthusiasm if you have camped in the right spots under favorable conditions — no tent flooding from torrential rains or bears breathing heavily outside your canvas. If you haven't camped, let's say you have the experience of a lifetime ahead of you.

1. **Why not camp in your own backyard for starters?** The neighbors won't mind, as long as you don't disturb their sleep. Set up your tent and sleep out. Summertime is best, of course. Even in fall and early winter, the adventure is feasible, as long as you have a warm sleeping bag and wear longjohns. Besides the fun of sleeping out, you will see your usual surroundings from a different perspective. Sounds and feelings will change.

2. **You don't have to go far to camp away from home, either.** Try a county park. Even the woods or the open field of a friendly farmer is great for pup-tenting. Company is safety, though. Don't try to go it alone. Nor should you camp too far from help, since emergencies do arise.

3. **If you have never spent a night on the beach and have a waterfront area available for overnight parking, you have a new thrill in store.** The stars will seem so close you will feel you can touch them. The sounds of wind, waves and night creatures will alert your senses and keep you awake long after you usually would be asleep.

4. **Camping with friends or family can become an ever-widening experience, eventually including international camps.** Read guidebooks, maps and camping site catalogs. Subscribe to camping magazines. Discover the opportunities open to you for camping in places from the Swiss Alps to Australian bush country. And in the meantime, head for the state and national parks sprinkled from coast to coast.

5. **Church camps offer a different type of camping — a peer group activity.** You're bunked in cabins or dormitories. You follow a busy schedule that includes Bible study, Morning Watch and Vespers, crafts and nature study, in addition to the usual sports and other recreational activities.

    Around nightly campfires, you sit and sing, tell stories and listen to messages that inspire you to live and give your best. You become aware of another dimension to camping that you would rarely experience while camping at some place other than a religious camp. There is a special warmth, companionship, involvement, joy and fulfillment. You are surrounded by beautiful people and counselors who care for you as a person. No one — absolutely no one, not even your best friend — can adequately describe the differences between a church camp and any other. You have to *experience* it.

CLIMB TO THE TOP

"Get high! But do it climbing cliffs," Randy challenged his classmates. He was talking about rock-climbing. And while exhibiting crampons and rope, he described the steep summits he had tackled in southwestern Pennsylvania.

"You don't have to climb the Sears Tower or the World Trade Building to get high," Randy continued. "Start around here. Any high rock ledge makes a good practice site.

"I got my basic training at the YMCA. The fellow who teaches the course has climbed the Sierra Nevadas. He says the going is really rough there. But the rules are the same wherever you rock-climb:

1. **"You learn *safety first* under a watchful guide.** Then you practice safety with every move you make."

2. **"It's no kid's game, either.** Our instructor allowed no one under 16 in the class he taught. He says most schools go along with that cut-off age — or maybe 18."

3. **"Equipment is furnished along with instruction.** After that, if you like the sport, as I do, you have to buy your own climbing irons and all."

4. **"Climbers have their own vocabulary, too:** 'cramponing techniques,' 'French-pointing,' 'rappelling,' 'belaying arrests' and 'prusik systems.'

   "Crampons are climbing irons. Belaying is making a rope secure by winding it around a cleat (belaying pin). For example: 'Belay on the cleat over there' is a direction used.

   "Rappelling is the method of moving down steep inclines or past an overhang by using a double rope. You secure this above you. Then place it around your body — usually under the left thigh and over the right shoulder. Let out the rope gradually in the descent.

"It's exhilarating," concluded Randy. "You conquer those rock-faced cliffs. You have power!"

Rock-climbing isn't for everyone, as Randy said. But maybe it's *your* high. How will you know until you try?

GO HANG-GLIDING

"Mom and I have signed up for hang-gliding instruction during summer vacation," Win announced to his classmates.

"Your mother!?" gasped one of his friends.

"Why not? She's the one who talked me into it. We can have adventure and thrills within a few miles of home. Want to join us?"

What is hang-gliding all about? "You jump off the top of a mountain, test the wind and have fun." That's how a hang-gliding American Cup winner explains it. (He took off from Lookout Mountain in Tennessee for his winning flight.) He also insists that sounding instruments help and that pilot training is necessary.

Hang-gliders say you feel like a bird — that actually, you emulate birds. These human fliers also warn you to think of gliding as dangerous, not as a soft sport. Serious injuries and death do occur. You must study the environment. Be aware of the flow of the air and the risks of being in the air.

Teen-agers who in 1970 were among the first launchers from high cliffs above the westward-facing beaches of California are instructors today. They train pilots to take total responsibility for what they do, to know and admit their limitations and to use their own judgment.

Since those first launchings, the sport has spread world-wide, with over 100,000 people having tried it. The FAI (Fédération Aeronautique Internationale) sponsors international competiton. The USHGA (United States Hang-Gliding Association) is a division of the larger unit.

Where can you learn more about hang-gliding? Read *The Hang-Gliding Book*, by William Bixby, David McKay Company, Inc., 1978.

Here, you will find descriptions of the components of gliders, methods of flying them, history and elements of flight theory, the sport's hazards, launching and landing areas and much, much more.

The pilot's personal word pictures of how he *feels* while gliding over Yosemite are breath-taking. You sense the oneness with the environment: no motor — only wind — and the skill and luck needed to stay in the air and then land safely.

For those of you who do not intend to attach yourselves to a wing and jump off a cliff, but want to read more about techniques, this second book is for you: *Hold in the Wind (Hang-Gliding and the Quest for Flight)*, by Hank Harrison, Bobbs-Merrill Co., Inc., 1979. This book is a simplified explanation. Included is a glider's glossary.

Happy flying — either by body or spirit.

JOIN A BICYCLE CLUB

Of course you have bicycled ever since you had training wheels. But how about a bicycle club? Why not join one and extend your activities? Here's how:

1. **Contact a bike club sponsor, such as** youth hostels, the YMCA or YWCA or city or county recreation departments.

2. **Find out what they do with their bicycling program.** Members may take trips together at designated times, for example. Some are casual trips on city bike trails through parks and along rivers. Longer rides, like the century (100 miles) and the metric century (62 miles), take you out into the country along carefully mapped routes on secondary roads.

   For example, the annual WAG bicycle ride, which begins and ends at Washington and Jefferson College, has a 50-mile covered bridge tour and a 15-mile history tour. And for the adventurous advanced bikers, they have a 100-mile trip.

   Bike club members often ride in bike-athons, such as Pedal for

Pets or *Ride for Epilepsy*.

Join a bike club for exercise, companionship and challenge — all outdoors. Try it. You'll like it.

MALL-HOP TO SEE FREE SHOWS

Of course you have been going to malls ever since your baby-stroller days. You window-shop. You browse. You buy. And occasionally, you stop to watch an act or program in progress near the central fountain, when you happen to be there at performance time.

However, by planning your mall trips expressly to see the shows, you will have free admission to some of the finest productions.

One mall, for example, billed five features within a single weekend. Karate demonstrations took place in the north wing at 2 and 4 p.m. A women's apparel show celebrated its grand opening with disco-dancing demonstrations at 3:30 and 7:30. In the south wing, the Radio Control Model Aircraft Club had a display. Throughout the central mall, a four-wheel drive club displayed more than 40 four-wheel drive vehicles, owned by dealers and individuals. Then on Sunday, Smucker's Jam Bluegrass Band played throughout the mall.

Take your choice or see everything offered in your nearest mall. If this fare does not suit you, or you still have time after viewing them, visit another mall — and another.

By noting the coming attraction announcements posted at the entrances, you can time your visits for activities that excite you. Some examples are:

- new automobile shows
- junior symphony concerts
- starving artists exhibits
- craft shows
- Junior Achievement fairs
- sports shows
- circus acts
- style shows

- recreation/vacation exhibits
- political candidates' appearances (including those of people running for the United States presidency)
- rock stars and beauty queens' personal appearances
- animal acts
- ice skating shows

Where else can you have such a potpourri of entertainment?

PICK FRUITS

Find yourself wild patches or cultivated rows of berries, trees or vines of fruit. And you will have a memorable experience of one kind or another. At least your peers the world over have found similar pursuits fun, profitable or surprising.

- Bonnie picked grapes one day, just for the fun of it, on a mountainside in the vineyards above the Chateau de Chillon. Armed with special scissors and a wooden bucket that had holes for handles, she (and 35 other young adults) climbed the steep slopes between rows of grapevines. In her assigned rows, Bonnie cut off each bunch of grapes and threw it in her bucket. Young men emptied her full buckets into a large wooden basket, where a crusher smashed the grapes.

  If Bonnie's basket was full before the young men returned to empty it, she made room for more grapes by smashing the contents with her foot — shoe and all. "This was fun," Bonnie related later. "But, oh, how I longed to tramp the grapes with my bare feet!"

  A tradition of the vineyard allows the young men who pick up the buckets to kiss the young woman who is picking grapes if she leaves a bunch of grapes on the vine — and gets caught. Bonnie received a kiss on each cheek.

- Near Traverse City, Michigan, Doris and Marge picked cherries to earn some money. Picking was fast and profitable. But even there, the unexpected happened. While Doris was picking from atop a 12-foot ladder, Marge jumped from the middle of the same ladder. Down fell the ladder, almost as if in slow motion. Doris landed on green onions that had been planted between the tree rows. Cherries scattered, but no one was hurt.

- In Florida, Tom and Jamie picked tomatoes for their family reunion of 16. Picking went quickly: they gathered 44 pounds in 10 minutes. The price was 10 cents a pound. But the farmer made a wager with Jamie: "Pay $3.50 for the lot without weighing. Or weigh the tomatoes and pay the going rate." Jamie chose to weigh, and lost 90 cents by doing so.

- And at Martha's Vineyard, Nancy and Debby picked wild blueberries to eat right then and there. They feasted abundantly — until they walked too close to a rookery. Then they fled from attacking sea gulls, Alfred Hitchcock-style.

Until you have an opportunity to pick grapes in Switzerland, why not start close to home base? Look in the daily newspaper's classified ad section during fruit seasons. Check advertisements for picking your own fruit.

If you use your own containers, you are not out the price of plastic and cardboard baskets. Wear old shoes (especially where irrigation is used).

You not only will have fun by following these opportunities, but you can save at least half the retail price, and sometimes much more. This way, you can help your family beat inflation. Or you can sell fruit at a profit to neighbors and friends.

RIDE A BLIMP

When that Goodyear blimp soars over you at football games, do you ever wish you could have a ride in the gondola? Fantastic? Maybe. Or perhaps you have to be numbered among the privileged to be invited. Then again, you may not, if you are at the lift-off when a radio talk show team embarks to broadcast from the sky. Strange bedfellows go with them. And you just might have the right persuasive pitch to convince the public relations officer that you should ride along with them. It has been done — even by a 9-year-old.

The ride is like nothing else. You hover over familiar landmarks. You get that strange mixed-up feeling when the pilot noses the ship down sharply to turn it around. Suddenly, your landing site becomes your ceiling. It's a topsy-turvy world.

For a unique experience, then, thumb a ride on a Goodyear blimp the next time it comes to town. And if you can't find a blimp, any hot-air balloon will do.

RIDE TO THE END OF THE LINE

"I remember when I was 7 or 8," Terry's grandfather told him. "I lived in New York City. And many a morning, I'd leave home with a nickel in my pocket. I'd use it to ride the subway all day."

The idea of going to the end of the line and back by subway, monorail or bus still sounds adventuresome. At least it chases away the "blahs" at any age.

Herb tried such a trip and found it amazingly stimulating. He was a shy, insecure 17-year-old who had never been outside of the county in which he was born (believe it or not). One day, though, he decided to venture out on his own. He bought a round-trip ticket to Washington, D.C. But when he arrived after five hours en route, he didn't leave the terminal. He was so confused by the city's noise and bustle that he jumped on the first homeward-bound bus. However, that trip completely changed his perspective and self-image. He had been to D.C.

As a city-dweller, you can explore your metropolitan map by bus, riding to distant points. As a suburban or village resident, you can ride to the next town, at least. In either case, you can turn your ride into a self-guided tour or a pleasant pastime. It's up to you.

But if you want to vitalize your trip, try these suggestions:

1. **Get a map ahead of time and follow the course of your journey as you bump along.**

2. **Note marked historical sites as they flash past.**

3. **Count the churches, schools, parks and hospitals.** Do their appearances depend on the neighborhood they're in? Of which do you find the most?

4. **Are you aware of socioeconomic boundaries?**

5. **What ethnic signs do you pass?**

6. **If you were a foreigner, what would be your overall evaluation of the segment of America through which you are passing?**

7. **What do you see that is beautiful?** architecture like the downtown cathedral, brand-new bank building or city arena? gardens, park entrances, civic statues? people?

8. **What features make your city or your area unique?**

9. **If you were to describe your trip in 25 words or less, what would you say?**

   A bus ride to the end of the line and back can be more than a ride. It can be an extraordinary eye-opener, full of intrigue and challenge.

SHOOT THE RAPIDS

Ready for white-water adventure? You may not be near enough to try the Rogue River or the churning waters of the Snake River through Hell's Canyon. But you are likely to have white waters nearby. At least seasonal rains often turn lazy rivers into turbulent cascades.

Check with friends who have ridden the rapids. They will eagerly share adventures and give you details as to where to go and when the waters are frothiest.

Consult state tourist bureaus, camping guides or recreational maps for the county if you need further information.

If you are unfamiliar with this sport, station yourself on a riverbank in a state or national park where kayaks and rubber rafts rush past. Note the power of the river. Watch the skilled and unskilled maneuvering of rafts, which scrape against boulders, miss upsets by inches or sometimes go aground in the shallows. Listen to the shouts of three or four on a single raft, zipping past with roller-coaster speed.

Note the equipment, most of which was probably rented at the park entrance — at least that is the usual routine. Look for life jackets and rafts or kayaks. Oh, sure, you saw some atop vans or being unloaded. But the young crowd settles for rentals.

The excitement is catching. You will want to be part of it. Watching is for older people. Once you venture down the local rivers, you will look for bigger, wilder rapids to ride. Set your sights high, and someday, you may experience the greatest white-water adventure of all — a journey down the Grand Canyon's Colorado River.

In the meantime, try any of the following white-water rivers, depending on your location, of course:

- the Nantahala, Chatooga or Ocoee, in Tenessee and the Carolinas
- the Salmon, in Idaho
- the Klamath, Deschutes or Middle Fork, in Oregon
- the Toulumne, Stanislaus or American, in California
- the Youghiogheny, in Pennsylvania, West Virginia and Maryland

TRY YOUTH-HOSTELING

Youth-hosteling is fun and exciting! I know. I've done it while bicycling 1,600 miles throughout the British Isles. I slept in castles, converted barns, thatched cottages and servants' quarters attached to Tudor manors. My overnight companions spoke several languages and shared experiences. All this was possible because I was an International Youth Hostel member.

Here in the United States, you need only an American Youth Hostel membership in order to use the simple, inexpensive overnight accommodations. Youth hostels are spaced within hiking and biking daily distance. You can sleep in a different hostel every night. You can stay more than one night at the same hostel, but you must vacate the premises during the day.

What do you need for youth-hosteling other than the membership card?

1.   A small fee is charged for each night's lodging.

2.   Take a sleeping sack.
This is not the usual sleeping bag (which takes more carrying space). You can make one by folding a sheet in half and stitching side and bottom. Leave the top open to snuggle down into. You may purchase one at national headquarters.

3.   Bring your own table service and dish towel.

With what accommodations do the hostels provide you?

4.   You can count on a bed (double-decker or cot) and blankets.

5.   Cooking facilities and utensils are there for you to use.

6.   Sometimes breakfasts are available (at least they are in England).

7. Whether you hike or cycle, travel light.

Hikers use backpacks for their luggage. Bikers sling saddlebags across carrier mounts atop their back wheels. They fasten smaller bags over front wheels. Seasoned hostelers take one change of clothing: a windbreaker, poncho or raincoat and a sunshade hat.

Youth-hosteling is an open sesame to thousands of miles of backpacking or bicycling pleasure. That's because you travel slowly enough to be part of your environment. You use secondary roads and specially constructed trails. Challenges are plentiful, too, like cycling 10 miles *downhill* against the wind.

Your rewards are numerous. The scenery, history and folk culture that enrich your days are matched only by the nights. Then the warm fellowship with other youth-hostelers envelopes you.

So join AYH and get involved in youth hostel activities. Write to:

American Youth Hostels
20 W. 17th Street
New York, New York 10011

Or if you live in a large city, look in the phone book for your local organization. Then make a phone call or visit the local office.

VISIT AN ART MUSEUM

Were you, by chance, one of the thousands of Americans who had a look at King Tut's gold and jewels? This road show of loaned objects from the tomb of Tutankhamen came from Cairo, Egypt. The artifacts had been buried with the king of the 18th dynasty in the 13th century B.C.

What a show to see! True, you had to be in one of the larger cities at the right time and stand in long queues. However, less earth-shaking exhibits make local stops. The point is that with a little effort on your part, you can see the world through art shows.

At Ringling Museum of Art in Sarasota, Florida, primitive wooden sculpture from Borneo drew hundreds of visitors (many of them teen-agers). The 133 carved figures stood in simulated tropical rain forests, etched in mystic light — a setting so effective that you felt you were actually visiting these Dyak tribesmen. The crude carvings depicted the rites of killing slaves to accompany their dead masters, for example.

In Pittsburgh, the Carnegie Museum hosts an international art show. It is always contemporary. It is splashy, controversial, spectacular.

You will find equally as exciting traveling exhibits near you. Watch for announcements and art reviews. Then go. See and enjoy!

VISIT A COURTROOM

Why settle for fictitious courtroom drama on television when you can see the *real* thing? Visit your county courthouse. Watch the action, whether it's a murder trial or a trial concerning a domestic squabble, traffic accident or a drug cache. Unravel plots. Figure out the verdict, as if you were on the jury.

Get involved in other people's lives, even though you are simply a spectator. Empathize! This is for real.

On your first courthouse visit, get acquainted with the layout of offices and chambers. Familiarize yourself with the roster of judges. Then walk into any courtroom where a case is being tried.

What you learned in civics courses will come to life here, for this is American law for ordinary people. The judge may be male or female, young or old. Lawyers may argue boisterously or speak so quietly that only judge and accused can hear. When it's a trial by jury, members will look as familiar as your next-door neighbors.

Savor the entire scene. You will be entertained, no doubt. You will also be wiser about legal problems after an hour or two in the courtroom. After all, to observe a trial is your prerogative as a United States citizen. Why not take a peek into those "halls of justice?"

VISIT HISTORICAL SITES

Sure, history can be a drag when you're studying for a quiz. On the other hand, it comes alive and grabs your imagination when you visit Andersonville, Fort Ticonderoga, Monticello or New Salem. The National Park Service maintains many such historic sites, perhaps near you. Some of you live in the cradle of American history. Others will have to seek and find.

Start, however, with sites which local, county or state historical societies have marked for you. Some, along main highways, you have spotted while passing too fast to read inscriptions. Others, bordering quiet side roads, you will have to hunt to find.

Journey with pad and pencil. Jot down plaque legends. Also diagram exact locations. Then combine your findings into an annotated map. This way, you will learn local history and discover data for special reports in history class, which may give you extra grade points. Others have plotted such maps, with those happy results.

For example, Sheri stopped, in one afternoon, at three sites maintained by the National Park Service. They were within a mile of each other, along old U.S. 40, west of Uniontown, Pennsylvania.

"I found not only General Braddock's grave, but also the site of his original burial, in the middle of Braddock Road. A trace of that trail is still visible," she told her classmates in an oral history report. She also described Fort Necessity and George Washington Tavern, once owned by our first president.

"History is all about you," Sheri said. "It can be a cave, a log cabin, an old well. Look for markers, or contact your historical society. They will put you on the trail."

VISIT LIBRARIES

It's incredible! What is? Your library! Get acquainted with city, county, college and state libraries in your own area and you'll soon discover for yourself that each one *is* incredible.

At the information desk, ask for a guided tour. Even when group tours are not scheduled, a library aide will show you through the maze of rooms and stacks. Or you can pick up a floor plan and guidebook which explains facilities and how to use the library.

A check list of many library contents and activities includes:

1. **Art reproductions.** These you can borrow on your library card. They're framed and ready to hang on your own walls. You can have a different picture for your room every three weeks.

2. **Audiovisual equipment.** You may use projectors, recorders or screens in the library, or take them out. They are also used by librarians for public showings.

3. **Business services and stock reports.** These are up-to-date and inclusive.

4. **Film collection.** Many big libraries have film departments with hundreds of reels for you to borrow. Some are educational; others, sheer entertainment. For example, you may check out a Charlie Chaplin film or a World War II documentary.

5. **Headphone listening areas.** Here, you can play tapes and records from the audiovisual files.

6. **Records and cassettes.** These also may be used in the library, in the earphone-listening area, or borrowed. For instance, you may take out recordings of *Westside Story*, a course in beginning Russian, country music or grand opera.

7. **Magazines, newspapers and phone books** from all over

the United States are on microfilm. And on microfilm-reading machines, you can read stacks of information.

8. **Talking books for the blind and physically handicapped, as well as large-print books and magazines,** are available. For example, along with the regular current *Reader's Digest*, you will find, in the magazine racks, a large-print copy.

9. **A newspaper clipping file.** This is handy to use when you have to do research for a school report.

10. **Out-of-town newspapers, copy machines, display cases, new-book shelves —** all these are there, in addition to the thousands of books and magazines for all ages.

11. **And if a bookmobile** is in the parking lot at the time you are touring, go inside it. It's neat and clean and every book is in place; the driver-librarian is ready to take books to outlying areas.

12. **Large city libraries (university libraries, too) have individual rooms or floors for particular fields,** each as large as a small-town library. There are sections on law, philosophy and religion, science, the arts and humanities (to name examples).

13. **The tour guide will show you closed-area stacks.** These are often for librarians only. To get books from here, you present the call number of the book you want at the circulation desk. A librarian or aide gets your book and sends it to the desk.

14. **Your guide also will explain the catalogue system.** Note that the same filing system is used in all libraries, your school library included. Books are listed by subject, author and title. Only the format is different. Some libraries use cards (the usual form). Others use film, big books or a television screen.

15.   Your guide will tell you about library services, too.
These will include the children's story hour, film showings and reference and telephone service.

For example, you can telephone the library, ask for the reference desk and ask any question about which you want information. The reference librarian will find the answer and return your call. Likewise, he or she will help you find answers to your questions when you are in the library.

A visit to each of the libraries near you is an open sesame to hours of pleasure and fulfillment, you will discover. So return again and again.

VISIT A MUSEUM

You weren't excited a bit when your mother took you to the museum to see a dinosaur. Remember? You were 5 and dinosaurs were already very real to you. You'd seen them in your storybooks.

But *everything* you see in museums isn't in storybooks. And a trip to a museum to see with teen-aged eyes will be quite different. Also, museums are now offering more and more wonders.

Take a natural science museum, for instance. It displays reptiles, insects, mammals, fish, shells and wildlife. Specifically, you will see warthogs, gnus and caribou placed in natural environmental dioramas to show what goes on in the Antarctic, the desert or rain forests.

Also, many amphibians, snakes and fish now are preserved in bottles. And some places, like Bean Museum at Brigham Young University, include live snakes and amphibians.

Even Walt Disney nature films are part of today's museum programs.

Sprinkled throughout the United States are literally thousands of museums worth traveling miles to see. Field Museum in Chicago is one. A unique one in Jacksonville, Florida, originally was referred to as the Children's Museum. Curators have dropped the "Children's" because teen-agers and adults enjoy it, too. You may be too big to slide through the ear of the giant face and come out through the mouth, but full-sized log cabins and a ship captain's quarters will pique your interest.

Check city and state museums nearest you. Then plan a visit for half a day at least — just to try it out.

VISIT A TELEVISION STATION

"That kitchen for the television bake-off is only a corner of the studio, not a real kitchen!" Dena observed after visiting a chef's show.

You, too, may be surprised by the size of props and sets. What gets done in overcrowded space will amaze you when you visit a television station. Every network station has at least one show with a live audience. This fact gives you a chance to see the action.

Call the station in advance. Find out if you need passes. Check on the exact time you must be in the studio. Arrive on time. Once the tally lights glow red on the cameras, you will not be admitted.

Most local broadcasting companies will also give you a tour of the entire facility, if you make arrangements in advance. The guide will show you the various monitors from which the producer picks the best camera shots. You will see properties and sets like Mr. Rogers' neighborhood in the Pittsburgh Public Broadcasting Station. TV jargon will be used, along with explanations of such words as "boom," "dolly," "fade-in," "minicam" and "videodiscs."

If you ask leading questions, the guide will give you the latest in television outreach, such as:

- Stations with access to a receiver can pick satellite transmissions from different places: news sources, movie studios, independent companies. In the past, network programming was the only choice.

- Cable television has become an around-the-clock news and sports service. And recent movies are offered for an extra price.

By 1990, 50 percent of American homes are expected to be wired for cable.

- Home video technology, which utilizes television sets and personal computers, is constantly being revolutionized.

Watching television at home will take on new dimensions after you have been on the set while a program is produced. You will have seen and talked with announcers, producers, actors, reporters and technicians. You will have tripped over the maze of electrical cords leading to camera dollies. You will know the actual size of what you see on your screen.

The romantic illusion will seem a little spoiled by reality. But that will be replaced by visions of fantastic future television encounters your guide suggested would be yours.

VISIT A THEME PARK

Are you a thrill-seeker? a roller-coaster addict? Then theme parks are for you. Bigger and more terrifying rides appear every year as park owners try to make their roller-coasters the most hair-raising in the world. Disney World officials bill their Space Mountain as "a winding, soaring race through space," for example. And the Loch Ness Monster at Busch Gardens in Virginia is billed as "the most insidious, awesome ride of its kind."

But theme parks are much more than roller-coasters. They are huge entertainment centers with international motifs: replicas of castles (Disneyland); landmarks (Eiffel Tower at King's Island, King's Mills, Ohio); shops, regional or ethnic foods; and costumed park attendants who contribute to the foreign or historic flavor.

Admission comes in different packages. Some parks have a general admission ticket you buy at the park entrance. This pays for everything except food and shopping items, as it does at Busch Gardens in Tampa, Florida, for instance. Disney World has one-, two- or three-day passes, to be used in place of individual tickets. Books of tickets for rides come in various denominations, according to the number of rides or exhibits you want to include.

And there are always the free goodies once you are inside the park: your favorite cartoon characters tickling you under your chin; parades of bands, antique cars and Disney animals; puppet shows; barbership quartet concerts; magic acts; exhibits and shows.

Perhaps one of the many theme parks scattered across the United States is near you. For instance, do you recognize any of these samplings? There are five "Six Flags" major parks, from Texas to New Jersey. Mariott has two "Great America" parks in Illinois and California. There are two Busch Gardens (mentioned above). The one in Tampa was the groundbreaker in the theme park concept. The "Dark Continent" opened in 1959. You can safari by monorail or steam locomotive, or sky-ride through or over the "Serengeti Plains," where wild African big game graze and roam. Or you can visit the "Congo" by boat. In Williamsburg, Virginia, the second Busch Gardens' theme is "The Old Country."

Some of these theme parks even have camping sites. That means you can take a mini-vacation there if you aren't within close enough range for a day trip.

MORE PLACES TO GO:

Attend an **antique show. Bike-pack.** Go **spelunking.** Go **surfing.** Organize **theater excursions** (to see legitimate plays and musicals). **People-watch. Picnic** in as many places as possible. **Take a trip,** staying with friends and relatives. Visit: a **coal mine, college campuses, craft shops, juvenile detention centers** or **prison farms,** local **industries** and **factories** that have tours, **newcomers** in your neighborhood, the **newspaper plant** while the paper is being printed, **special education classes, travel agencies** and **youth centers** in other cities. **Water ski.**

Stretch Your "Know-how"

ACT, DESIGN SCENERY AND CREATE LIGHTING EFFECTS

Join an acting workshop and you have lots of fun ahead of you. You'll have opportunities, too, without having to be an actor the rest of your life.

You will have to do all sorts of strange things, though, to break down inhibitions. Expect to climb chairs, do sit-ups, cry, laugh and scream. After that warm-up, you will act out scenes from plays. In time, your confidence will be built up to where you can recite memorized lines before an audience and create a character by losing your own identity in that of another person.

To accomplish all this, join a theater group. This may be a community theater, a summer barn theater, your own high-school thespian club or a religious drama group directed by a professional. Such groups usually meet regularly and invite professionals from every phase of the theater to share their expertise.

Sometimes, you can attend these meetings without joining the group, since the public is invited when out-of-towners perform. And some theater groups conduct special sessions for high-school students.

You learn by doing and observing. You get walk-on parts in current productions. You will learn all about the theater by watching actors, technicians, stage designers and makeup artists at work. Just being backstage exposes you to the life-pulse of the legitimate theater — an exciting, fanciful world.

- For example, Phil, a high-school sophomore, is with McKeesport Players (Pennsylvania), a civic group. He says he never had enough time for the activities open to him.

  In the summer, he sets up the stage and acts in a roving children's theater group that performs on the back of a truck at playgrounds. In the winter, he helps with high-school plays and works on the civic theater stage crews. "I also get a bit part now and then," he says.

- Another teen-ager, Laura Dee, with three years' experience in civic theater, won a summer workshop fellowship at Bucknell University. All expenses were paid.

- And still a third student from the same high school placed among the limited number of those admitted to Northwestern University's high-school workshop. His eligibility was due to school and church drama experience.

None of these young people is likely to see his or her name on a marquee. But they have found a challenging outlet for their time and energy. You can, too! Watch for notices in the paper and on bulletin boards. Hound your drama teacher for information, or make direct contact with a theater group.

BE A BIBLIOMANIAC

That means "hooked on books." Whether or not you go that far, try collecting books for a hobby that pays off.

The search for old books can be intriguing. You may want to specialize in first editions; in books by a single author, like James Michener; or in books on a particular subject. The owner of a rare-book shop says the current demands are for books on Americana, cookbooks, illustrated books, 19th century children's books, circus books and books by Edgar Allan Poe.

At least test your interest in old books. Visit a second-hand-book store. Or browse through a rare-book shop, if your town has one. The strange scent of aging leather bindings and dusty, musty pages may entice you to start your own collection — be it fairy tales or illustrated fashions. Then again, the smell may repulse you.

You may be lucky enough to have a relative with an attic full of old books. If so, ask for permission to hunt. With luck, you might find a rare volume that would later help pay your college tuition. You might also find a subject to follow up, like Jim did when he found two old hymn books, copyrighted in 1846 and 1934.

Other sources for old books are rummage sales or flea markets. Books go for just pennies each, sometimes. Margarite bought a first edition of *A Farewell to Arms* for a quarter at a garage sale. When she had a rare-book shop owner evaluate it, he offered her $150.

But whether or not you sell books for a profit, a book collection opens doors to the past, present and future. You can make friends of characters within the books and while looking for old copies.

- Al says he has more friends in books than he does in real life.

- Barbara and Stuart met in a bookstore. "I liked her looks and the book she was looking at, so I struck up a conversation," Stuart said. "Now we are married."

BE A SPECIALIST

None of his classmates could stump Chris on any statistics, past or present, concerning the Cincinnati Reds. He was a walking computer. In other words, the Reds were his specialty. And as a result, he drew awe and admiration from his peers.

You, too, can become a specialist in anything you turn into an obsession. Learn all you can about one subject, such as:

- professional golf
- American Indians
- wilderness survival
- trains
- maps
- blue laws
- spirituals
- United States presidents
- gourmet cooking
- fishing
- baseball trivia
- religious publications for young people
- astronomy

- the history of the Olympics
- space flights

Once a subject fascinates you, the accumulation of facts, stories and statistics grows quite naturally.

BRUSH UP ON ETIQUETTE

No, that isn't an old-fashioned word. We have modern etiquette, too. So don't let the term turn you off. It's not necessarily stuffy procedures, practiced only by high society of bygone days. It affects you, too. For instance:

- How do you act at a wedding or a funeral?

- What is appropriate dress for these and other occasions?

- If you are a young man, do you know what is expected of you when taking a young woman on a date?

- As a young lady, do you know what to do or not do toward paying expenses of a date?

- How do you respond when introduced to older people?

- How do you introduce your teen-aged friend to your minister?

- How do you act during a job interview?

Even in our present free-wheeling society, etiquette is important. Why? Because it implies thoughtfulness toward others. It is a set of suggestions that help us get along with each other more smoothly. And it is flexible, changing with the times.

Therefore, any effort you make to learn how to do things the acceptable way surely will be a plus for you. Your most recent guide is Letitia Baldrige's revision of *Amy Vanderbilt Complete Book of Etiquette* (Doubleday, October, 1978).

While brushing up on the latest social fashions, you may enjoy peeking into an Emily Post etiquette book of the past. (Your public library will have some.) Note changes in social customs since she wrote, as well as time-tested customs we still follow. Discover why certain customs originated. For example, you will find that the man walked on the curb side of the sidewalk while escorting a lady. Why? To prevent her from being splashed with mud by passing prancing horses.

As teen-agers, many of you tend to resist rules — especially those established for behavior in polite society. Nonetheless, they exist for your benefit, believe it or not. And particularly if you are aiming for life as an official or professional in the next few years, what you learn now will help you later. It's just a fact of living: you can't always do what you want to do, when and where you want to, the way you want to do it.

"Worst luck!" you say. But is it? Not when the other person is doing his or her thing in the wrong place at the wrong time. Agreed?

COLLECT AUTOGRAPHS

First, let's define what we mean by "autographs," in terms that professionals use: "anything written by oneself." The word comes from two Greek words, "auto" and "graphos," and means "self-writing."

Therefore, a signature is an autograph. But any single word, or thousands of words, written by oneself is an autograph. Of course, the signature is all-important, and without its attachment to letters, notations or whatever, that material loses its identity and significance.

Nonetheless, according to the *Stern and Dale book of World Autographs*, the most important part of an autograph is its contents. Other autograph values are length, condition, significance (to sender or receiver, if it is a letter), rarity and desirability (marketability). For instance, historical autographs are gaining in popularity.

In collecting, you can generalize or specialize. In other words, collect anything or everything that appeals to you, and that you think might have intrinsic value. Or concentrate on a single period in history or on members of one profession, like scientists or sports figures.

Assuming you have very little money with which to start your collection, find autographs yourself. Don't buy from other collectors in the business.

Write to living people. Ask for their autographs whenever you can push pen and pad in front of celebrities you see in person. You may have to be a bit brash to get results. But always be courteous, of course.

For autographs of the past, haunt antique shops, junk shops and old bookstores. Go to estate sales, where house contents are sold. And don't neglect autographs that may be hidden in your grandparents' storerooms. Flyleaves of old books, diaries, yellowed letters tucked into old Bibles — all are potential sources.

Do you need more stimuli to seek autographs? Then scan the signatures found in the Stein and Dale book mentioned above — 1,600 of them, including those of Joan of Arc (1430), Napoleon, Columbus and Aaron Burr.

Combine autograph-collecting with hand-writing analysis and you double the excitement of either hobby.

COLLECT POSTERS

James collects posters of Porsches. Brenda just added the latest popular music star to her poster galaxy. Brit collects pictures of rock stars to match the albums he spins.

And why not? Posters are exciting, easy to collect and almost always conversation pieces. You can even have a blown-up poster of yourself made to order. At the rate they are flooding the market, you would think they were going out of style. Not so, if history proves anything. Posters have been around a long time.

The first political slogan and cartoon posters appeared in the middle 19th century. Several are on display in the old Ford Theater Museum in Washington, D.C.

Then along came the French artist, Henri de Toulouse-Lautrec, with his striking poster designs. His lithographs of Yvette Guilbert immortalized this French *danseuse* and café singer.

Uncle Sam and the armed forces joined the poster business during World War I. James Montgomery Flagg designed 45 hard-hitting recruiting posters.

Still another poster artist was Howard Chandler Christy, whose "Christy girls" made him famous. These buxom beauties became his hallmark.

People collect posters of many kinds. For example:

- Political enthusiasts amass party placards that clutter America's crossroads during every election.

- Sports fans collect posters of sports personalities.

- Movie, television and music buffs concentrate on their favorite stars or groups.

Others specialize in wildlife, the Olympic games, travel, theatrical coming attractions and advertising posters for anything that is sold.

You, too, can choose your favorite subject — or have a potpourri of many interests. You may start your assemblage by begging. Contact the movie theater manager as he or she takes last week's coming attraction posters out of the showcases. Or ask a travel agent for outdated trip signs. Help yourself to the political telephone pole posters that are still intact after an election. Get permission to strip your school corridors of announcement posters, once the events are over. These will give you an animated account of your high-school days — plays, musicals, sporting events, international nights, elections, pep rallies, contests.

If you time your appeal just as the store manager is changing seasonal decor, you can get holiday and special events posters free. This goes for malls, civic centers, airplane and bus terminals, hotels, churches — wherever seasonal posters are used.

Other posters, you will have to buy, of course. They are for sale from Disney World, the local museum or religious bookstores, depending on your subject. Their prices span from a dollar to thousands, if they are collector's items.

A word of warning, though: *do not fold posters*, advise the experts. Once they are creased, they fall apart more readily. Store them flat. Hang them on your bedroom walls (one atop the other, if necessary). Stack them flat under your bed, maybe?

COLLECT WORDS

Fred's hobby is collecting words. It started when he received his SAT score. His weakest area was word usage. And although he was a semi-finalist and two Ivy League colleges had offered him four-year scholarships, Fred figured he must build up his vocabulary. He set a goal of five new words a day. "That was my New Year's resolution," he explained.

In typical Fred-style, he worked out a detailed attack. He wrote all new words (that he heard, saw or read) in the back of his assignment book, which he carried in his pocket. When he had time, he transferred the words into a loose-leaf notebook, one to a page.

He wrote all the meanings beneath the word. At the bottom of the page, he wrote five sentences using the word correctly. At the back of the notebook, he recorded each word alphabetically, along with the page number on which it appeared. (He indexed, in other words.)

You may have a shorter system, as Ruth did. She faithfully cut out word quizzes from the newspapers. After checking her multiple-choice answers, she memorized correct meanings for those she missed.

If this daily exercise is too much for you, why not follow Jody's scheme? She writes down all new words she hears. She looks up their meanings and records them in a small notebook. Then she whips out the list and gets acquainted with two or three while riding the bus or waiting for an appointment. "That turns boredom into new words," Jody says.

ENROLL IN SUMMER PROGRAMS

What's there to do? Almost every city and many small towns have the answer. They offer youth all sorts of activities, from building sand castles for prizes to day camps, field trips and theater workshops. Usually, all you have to do to qualify is register and sometimes pay a small fee.

Take St. Petersburg, Florida, for example. A young resident there has city, county and state recreational activities from which to choose. The city's Department of Leisure Services offers junior and senior high-school students a complete summer program for a small registration fee. There is softball, volleyball, drama, archery, gymnastics, football and swimming.

Also, the Pinellis County Science Center sponsors canoeing and rafting trips, mountain and Appalachian trail hikes, underwater exploration, metal crafts and marine biology.

The Florida Division of Forestry has an outdoor excursion for sixth- to eleventh-graders, too. For a weekly rate, youths live in bunkhouses and learn how forests affect their lives. This environmental study takes place in Withlacoochee State Forest (in central Florida) and at Blackwater State Park (northeastern Florida).

These government-sponsored summer programs are often based on a sliding fee scale. You're charged according to your economic resources. Private programs, however, are more expensive.

Still using St. Pete for an example, Eckerd College has a summer theater workshop for young people (12-15 years). There, you can learn to mime, act and work with puppets. Tuition is paid by the week, and also includes field trips and films.

Various religious denominations have conference or state camps for teen-agers. Closer to home are district camps. Larger churches sponsor their own camps or camping periods at the denomination campgrounds. Contact your local church office or youth director for information and registration blanks. Youth groups often earn money to pay part of the individual costs.

Your own high school has summer classes that challenge. You can learn to type in six weeks, with or without credit for graduation. You can concentrate on a foreign language or computer training.

And don't overlook the many programs offered teen-agers by colleges in your area. For tops in debate, go to Georgetown University in Washington, D.C., or Northwestern University School of Speech, Evanston, Illinois. For journalism, Ohio University in Athens, Ohio, ranks superior, say those who have been there. Hundreds of other colleges have one- and two-week programs in science, dramatic arts and sports. You name it; some college is probably offering it.

Trade schools give similar teen-age workshops in electronics and broadcasting.

Hundreds of things to do during summer vacation are already planned for you. But you have to make contact. Sign up at the proper time and place. In fact, early registration is a must for many of these programs. The popular ones have limited space. So plan your summer before the snow melts! Enjoy!

EXPAND YOUR RELIGIOUS KNOWLEDGE

"God is a straitjacket, an adult boogeyman." So stated an atheist in a radio talk-show interview.

How would you have reacted to such a description of God? Would you have phoned in and told him off? Many people did. They were angry, hostile, even frightened to have such ideas coming into their homes.

You may not meet an atheist face-to-face. But every day, you brush up against fellow students who think differently about religion than you do. They have been brought up in other environments. Some are as hostile toward your beliefs as those callers were toward the atheist. And someday, you may be put on the spot to declare your faith and your beliefs, as candidly as the atheist did his. Are you ready?

Probably not, for the teen-age years are a time for questioning, evaluating and investigating. And that's as it should be. You are still growing, still reaching out . . . and up.

A young camp counselor who has exposed himself to religious seminars, debates and much study, suggests the following guidelines for religious growth:

1. **Hang on to your religious heritage until you are sure another viewpoint is better for you.**

2. **Be tolerant of other interpretations, other faiths.**

3. **Indulge in Bible-reading, worship services, talks and discussions by religious leaders.**

4. **Question.**

5. **Keep an open mind.**

6. **Be willing to see the good in other people's beliefs.**

7. **Pray for yourself and others.**

8. **Study church history, Bible history and other world religions, like Hinduism, Islam and Buddhism.**

9. **Be loving — not irritating, dogmatic or argumentative — when talking religion with others.**

10. **Be humble.** You won't have all the answers — ever. And some will change as you experience more.

    And, I would add, *enjoy!* Religion should be life-giving, life-saving, life-fulfilling!

    Right now, try writing out for yourself exactly what you believe about God, creation, the universe, Jesus, prophets, churches, the Bible, etc. Use your own language, not words and phrases you have memorized from catechism or Sunday school. Admit what you aren't sure of. And if it helps you know where you stand, list what you *don't* believe at this time.

Put your creed in a safe place where you can look at it from time to time. Add to or scratch out as you grow in religious knowledge. After all, you don't want to keep a kindergarten picture of God when you are 16, do you?

This activity can be on-going and challenging.

GET ACQUAINTED WITH BALLET

Nothing is sissy about ballet. Otherwise, the teen-aged audience would not have been so enthusiastic. They cheered and applauded the athletic-looking dancers as they took their bows at midcourt in the high-school gymnasium. A profesisonal dance theater group had been demonstrating jazz steps and classical ballet.

A few years ago, though, ballet was not that well received in America. The public preferred shoulder pads and tennis rackets to leotards and toe shoes. Then along came live ballet from Lincoln Center, Kennedy Center and even the White House, televised for millions to see. As a result, more and more young people — including males — are taking ballet lessons. Ballet is being included in public school art enrichment courses. And physical education courses in some schools now contain instruction in basic dance steps.

You, too, can get involved, for the enjoyment and exercise ballet offers. Challenge your boy- or girlfriend to join a class with you at the YMCA or YWCA, or as an after-school, extracurricular activity. Any exposure to ballet at this time will add to your appreciation of future television or community theater presentations.

INTERN IN A PROFESSION, TRADE OR BUSINESS

"Senior Career Month" is an intern program at Norwin Senior High School (Pennsylvania) every May. The plan excuses students from regular classes if their grades are good enough. They still have to submit planned homework. And they are not excused from finals.

Each of these seniors who elects to participate in the program spends regular working hours with a professional or business person. The student observes, questions and emulates. Supervised work is definitely expected, too. These apprentices do not get paid. However, they do get half a credit, a passing or failing grade and a critique of themselves and the program.

Why not seek such an internship for yourself during summer vacation? Find a professional in an occupation that interests you: pharmacy, ministry, law, medicine, city planning, merchandising, auto mechanics, cosmetology or aviation. Persuade that person to let you watch, listen and do the small tasks that will help you understand the job.

Expect no pay. But once your services are helpful, you likely will get some remunerative thank-you. You learn by doing. And in doing, you find out whether or not this is what you want for your life's work.

LEARN ABOUT POLITICS

Do you know the names of your state senators? In what congressional district are you living? Where would you go to vote? Who is your lieutenant governor?

Be informed about politics, voting and legislation. Get information about issues concerning your community, such as raising the millage for school taxes, issuing bonds for a new sewer system or improving law enforcement. Then after researching the subject, *take a stand.*

If you haven't already had an American history, civics or problems of democracy course, bone up on these subjects. Borrow a textbook and read. Audit class sessions when students discuss registration, absentee voting and different kinds of elections.

Telephone the city hall or county courthouse or Democratic or Republican party headquarters for similar information. Send for the League of Women Voters' nonpartisan pamphlet, put out especially for students. Attend political meetings and talk with the candidates present. Telephone city officials and school board members to find out how they stand on bond issues or foreign affairs.

Scan the newspapers for announcements of open meetings, rallies, demonstrations and dinners. Crash them when necessary. You can always find standing room. This way, you gain information beyond the spoon-fed television and radio diet.

And once your adrenalin flows faster, offer your help. Distribute flyers. Get on a telephone committee. Usher at rallies.

In other words, expand your involvement. And perhaps you will want to run for office. Be the mayor of your town. Get on the school board. Other teen-agers are filling these posts. Why not you?

LEARN HANDWRITING ANALYSIS

Todd fell into step with his English teacher as she raced from one class to the other. "I hope you don't mind," he panted. "But I've been analyzing your handwriting, Miss Clark. You know, your comments on my compositions?"

"A graphologist, are you?"

"Sort of. An amateur. But I'm saving my money to take a correspondence course. I've studied every book in the library on the subject."

"And what did you learn about your English teacher?"

"Well, you cross your *t's* way above the letter, you know."

"Yes, I'm aware that I do, especially when I'm in a hurry," Miss Clark said.

"Well, if the bar is above the center of the letter, that indicates enthusiasm. The length of the bar shows you are forceful and follow through. Also, the slant of your handwriting — to the right — shows you are emotionally expressive."

"You have learned your lesson well, Todd."

"And you dot your *i's* immediately above the letter. That means you have a good memory."

"And pay close attention to details," Miss Clark added.

"Aw, you know all about handwriting," Todd said.

"Why not? Stop in my room after school. I'll lend you a book on graphology."

"I'll take you up on that. Thanks. There's the bell. I have to backtrack to physics class."

According to experts in the field, you, too, can unlock secrets about yourself. You can even keep track of your own moods and health, they say — like taking your own pulse. If anything is wrong, your handwriting patterns change. As Todd points out, the *slant* of your handwriting indicates emotions. If it leans to the left, you tend to be reticent — an introvert. Straight up and down indicates you are calm and collected. And the more your writing slants to the right, the more of an extrovert you are.

Also, letter size supposedly measures energy and enthusiasm. The larger the letters, the more you have of both. Low-crossed *t's* show a lack of self-confidence.

Of course, you have to take all handwriting characteristics together for a complete picture of yourself. But any good graphology book will give you full information.

Today, people take the subject seriously enough for industrial and commerical employers to analyze applicants' handwriting as another indication of character traits.

LEARN ANOTHER LANGUAGE

Learn Chinese and qualify for future international jobs.

That's why Marla joined the Army. "To learn Chinese," she kids. Because of proficiency in foreign languages while in high school, she qualified for a Chinese language concentration program. "And concentrate, I do," Marla told underclassmates when she came home on leave. "That's all we do day in and day out — including table talk at meals. Chinese takes twice as long to learn as French."

Marla was right in her comparison. If you have average intelligence, you will spend 480 hours to reach survival level in a new language, according to the Foreign Service Institute's School of Language Studies. Survival means getting yourself fed, clothed and sheltered in a foreign country. That is six semesters if translated into foreign language classes in high school (one hour a day, five days a week, 18 weeks per semester).

To achieve the same level of survival takes 240 hours of Western European language study.

Whether you learn Chinese or any other language, you have several options open to you:

1. **If you enroll in a crash course like Berlitz, you learn in a hurry.** A native-speaking teacher bombards you with the language nine hours a day for two to six weeks, if you are in a rush. Or you can take private or semi-private classes for a recommended minimum of 30 lessons. Aimed for international business people, Berlitz (or any other commercial school) charges a sizable fee. Provided you have the funds and really want to learn a new language, Berlitz claims it can teach practically any living language.

2. **Another option is night or weekend classes offered by your own school district under its adult education program.** For example, Arlington, Virginia, public schools have had as many as 14 different language courses at one time.

3. **Look to a college or university near you for Saturday classes open to qualified high-school students.**

4. **Another approach is to find a foreign-speaking person in your community to tutor you.** For instance, Stacy asked the foreign exchange student from Norway to teach him Norwegian. In exchange, Stacy helped Erik with English. At least one foreigner is living in your community — students, young adults on work visas, foreign wives or husbands. Any one of them could teach you.

5. **And don't forget your own relatives.**
Bruce's great-grandmother came to America from Sweden when she was 18. Immediately, she learned to speak English. For years, she had spoken Swedish only with her own generation of the family — until Bruce asked for help.

   "After graduation, I'm going to Sweden. Will you teach me Swedish so I can get around the country easier?" Great-grandma was pleased to teach Bruce "survival" Swedish.

6. **Still another way to learn a foreign language is to teach yourself by means of records and cassettes.** You can borrow such courses from your school or community library. Use your card, just as you would for a book. The recordings come complete with phrase and grammar books. Or you may prefer to buy a beginning home-study package. Berlitz, Linguaphone, Assimil and Cortina are some of the marketing companies.

   The compensations for learning another language are well worth the work involved. The world accepts English, to be sure. But to really get to know people in a foreign land, speak their language!

LEARN A NEW SKILL, LIKE SIGN LANGUAGE

"Talk to the Deaf" was the title of a sign language class for beginners at Trinity Lutheran Church of the Deaf in Wilkinsburg, Pennsylvania. Anyone could enroll for a 12-week course. This is one example of opportunites given the public to learn sign language.

- Debby taught herself. She picked up a few of the motions by mimicking a deaf friend. Then she found a book on sign language in the library and taught herself.

- Bill learned the entire symbol language from a piano tuner under whom he apprenticed. Lip-reading thwarted him when the speechless tuner formed words with his mouth. So almost out of the necessity to communicate with his boss, Bill concentrated on motions. Now Bill can talk with the deaf wherever he meets them.

You can, too. Debby says it's like a foreign language. "Once you have learned it, you have a passport into another world."

LEARN SCUBA DIVING

Do you see yourself plunging deep down into the tepid turquoise waters of the Caribbean? Below the sun-splashed surface, wild-colored fish dart past your mask. You are surrounded by exotic sea creatures — giant starfish, great green turtles and manta rays. You gather conch for supper, or explore a sunken Spanish galleon.

If you are an experienced scuba diver, such fantasies can come true, sooner or later. And if you are not yet initiated into this *in* sport, you can be — no matter how far you are from ocean reefs.

1. **Sign up at your nearest YMCA for an introductory scuba diving course.**

2.   Line up in full gear (loaned or rented).

3.   Plunge into the YMCA pool.

- At least that's how Nels describes the beginners' class he is in at the Greensburg, Pennsylvania, YMCA. However, it is not all just fun and games, he admits. He's learning essentials, such as care of equipment, diving physics and decompression problems.

- Another high-school student has completed a similar basic program at an Ohio YMCA. And she has graduated from pool to quarries for more advanced instruction. In the deeper waters, she is learning how to handle underwater emergencies.

  "It sounds crazy," Ann says, "learning scuba diving in a swimming pool! Mine quarries make a little more sense. Anyway, I have qualified instructors. I've learned the basics of this underwater sport. And I'll soon be ready to dive in far-away places. Hawaii, maybe? Or the Fuji Islands? Why not? The whole world's out there to explore."

LEARN WINDSURFING

Have you tried this "purest form of sailing?" Boardsailing, also called windsurfing, originated only a few years ago, and has challenged young people ever since.

1.   What is windsurfing?
Although called a combination of sailing and surfing, windsurfing involves skills of its own. You use your body to hold up the mast and manage the sail. Thus, you become part of the craft. The position of the sail, angle of the mast, placement of your feet and heading of the board all affect your ride.

2.   What does boardsailing equipment include?

- A plastic-coated hull, filled with foam. This weighs 42 pounds,

is 12′ long and can be carried under your arm. It is so stable that it won't flip over when you climb onto it from the water.

- The 14-foot mast has a teakwood or aluminum boom circling it. This is your handrail while managing the angle of sail and mast. And the mast (attached to the hull at a universal joint) is held upright only by you, the sailor. When you release it, mast and sail fall flat into the water, but stay afloat.

- The daggerboard is slipped through the hull, to keep it from turning sideways on the water when the wind pushes on it.

- At the rear of the board (hull) are fins that project into the water to stabilize that end.

3.　How do you windsurf?

First of all, you just need water, not waves. With mast and sail lying flat in the water, you tug on the rope, which is tied to the mast. Finally, you pull it upright, and with some difficulty, you will stand on your wobbly board. Once you turn the sail to catch the wind, you can lean back toward the water and pull the boom with you. If the wind is strong, you will race across the water at incredible speed.

LISTEN

"My parents never listen to me," complained Dennis.

"Maybe so," said his girlfriend. "But do you listen to them?"

"Hey, whose side are you on?"

"Both, I guess. We've done a month-long research project on listening in communications class, and I'm suddenly aware that we teenagers don't listen, either. We made out a check list," Ruby explained.

"Now you sound like a school teacher."

"So you turn me off. And you're proving a point."

"What point?"

"You stop listening when a subject comes up that you don't like. We all do this sometimes. Do you want me to ask you the check-list questions, Dennis?"

"Fire away. I see you have your notebook open."

1. **"Do you look directly in the eyes of the person you are speaking to?"** asked Ruby.

   "You mean I should? Sure I do, when it's a gorgeous brunette asking the questions."

   "Be serious, Dennis. Eye contact shows your interest."

2. **"Do you use facial reaction,** such as lifting an eyebrow or smiling, to indicate your concern?"

   "Sure. Can't you see my ears wiggle?"

3. **"Do you empathize?** Do you stand in the other person's shoes; see and feel what he or she sees and feels?"

   "She, in this case," Dennis prompted.

4. **"Do you try not to interrupt the speaker?"**

   "You're the interrupter, Ruby, not me."

   "I know. That's one of my worst faults — anticipating what is going to be said and helping out."

5. **"Next, do you try to shut out distractions?"**

   "Like that plane buzzing overhead? That's impossible."

6. **"Do you concentrate on what is being said — even when the speaker is boring?"**

   "You're not boring, Ruby, even when asking dumb questions."

7. **"Do you refrain from faking attention?"**

   "You've got me there. I'm a master attention-faker, especially in algebra class."

8. **"Do you still listen when you don't understand the subject?"**

"No."

9. **"Do you keep your prejudices from showing?"**

"Not when it comes to women's lib!"

10. **"Do you keep cool when the speaker gets argumentative?"**

"No. I have to get in the act."

11. **"Do you ask questions and make comments while listening, without passing judgment or criticizing?"**

"I guess not. I've been a bit sarcastic while you've been reading this check list. Sorry."

12. **"Are you open-minded enough to recognize the other person's right to his or her point of view, even when you do not agree?"**

"That, I am — open-minded."

13. **"Do you listen to how the person feels as expressed in body language and voice inflection?"**

"I sure watched your body language, Ruby. It's beautiful."

"That's the quiz. Thanks, Dennis, for staying with it."

"I see what you mean, Ruby, when you asked if I listen to my parents. I don't."

The next time you are looking for something to do, seek out someone who needs to be listened to, like that kid you've been avoiding because he talks too much. Practice these listening skills while he rambles on. Or listen to your brother. Hear him out. What is he telling you through his body language?

Can you empathize?

Concentrate on one skill at a time, and gradually, you will improve your listening. In the end, you may be the most popular teen-ager in school. Everyone likes to be listened to.

ORGANIZE A WRITERS' CLUB

Do you like to write? Have you secret publishing ambitions? Then write! And send out your scripts.

Subscribe to *Writer's Digest* or *The Writer*. Get your hands on a copy of this year's *Writer's Market*. These publications will spell out the mechanics for preparing your manuscript, and how and where to send it. Study markets throughly. Study at least six issues of the magazine to which you plan to send your script. Slant your material for that publication.

Mail original copy, with a self-addressed stamped envelope enclosed. If your manuscript is accepted, congratulations! You have talent — or good timing. If your story is not accepted, expect vague, printed rejection slips. Editors are busy. They haven't time to write personal critiques.

And that's where a writers' club fills the void. Find a couple of other writer friends who produce, not just talk about writing someday. You will keep up your enthusiasm for writing when surrounded by those who are also eager to sell. If they, too, have the urge, dedication and fortitude to withstand constructive criticism — and give it — you have the makings of a helpful relationship.

Meet regularly, once a month. Require a new manuscript from each member whenever you meet. This will keep you writing. Have manuscripts read aloud (either by the writer or another member). Orally discuss the manuscripts' merits and areas that can be improved. Be impersonal. Be thorough. Be honest. Also, share other writing information on rejection slips (a sign your manuscript is active), editors' comments and writing tips. Celebrate sales.

Now that you have the idea for a writers' club exciting your imagination, why not enthuse your classmates who have shyly admitted that they write, too. You won't need to persuade. If they are serious, they will eagerly join you. Who knows? You may be helping to blast off a best-seller!

SEARCH FOR SCHOLARSHIPS AND LOANS

You can save yourself a mint in money by being scholarship- and loan-smart. If you plan to go on to college or trade school after you graduate, get busy now. Learn all you can about the free hand-outs and low-interest loans.

1. **Can you get financial aid from federal programs?** Contact your school guidance counselor to find out requirements. Realize that these government loans have lower interest rates and longer repayment schedules than those any commercial bank will give you or your parents. At least get your hands on a loan application. Read it carefully, and then share the information with your parents.

    The current application for Federal Student Aid (AFSA) includes five programs. (Your public library has free copies of "The Student Guide" booklet and this application blank) Fill out this form and send to:

    > Federal Student Aid Programs
    > P.O. Box 4101
    > Iowa City, Iowa 52244

    Presto! You will be considered for any one of these financial aids, if you meet requirements:

    - Pell Grants. These are not loans, so you do not have to pay them back.

    - Supplemental Educational Opportunity Grants (SEOG). You do not have to pay these back, either.

- College Work-Study (CW-S). You earn money while attending school.

- National Direct Student Loans (NDSL). This is a low-interest loan which you must pay back. This loan is made to you through the financial aid office of the school you will attend.

- Guaranteed Student Loans (GSL). A bank or credit union loans you money at low interest — also to be paid back.

  Another form you may pick up at the library is not for everybody: "Special Condition Application for Federal Student Aid." You can use this application if your family's financial status has changed for the worse, due to death, separation or divorce or loss of a job or benefits.

2. **Write to your state scholarship agency in your state's capital city.** Ask about the State Incentive Grant Program (SSIG). The federal government matches state grants to students in all 50 states. In the same letter, inquire about any other state loans.

3. **Write to colleges that interest you, asking for details about their scholarship and loan programs.** The bigger the school, the more financial aids are offered — especially in work-scholarships. Your school library will have catalogs with some financial facts and addresses. Occasionally, you may have personal contact with a university recruiting or admissions officer who visits your school. Ask that person for advice.

4. **To widen your self-help resources, look into the work-study programs offered by more than 1,000 colleges and universities.** These plans require you to study and attend classes full-time for a term. Then you alternate with a full-time working term — at a career-oriented job, for which you are paid. These schools report that their graduates get better jobs and earn more during their lifetimes. Whether or not this is true, cooperative educational programs are worth investigating.

5. **Other financial aids may be right under your nose.**

- Because you live in a particular housing plan, for instance, you may be eligible for scholarship dollars.

- Because your father or mother is employed by a national or international corporation (like Pittsburgh Glass), you may automatically be in line for a scholarship. Your grades and class standing count. Your financial need is also a consideration.

- Many of the organizations to which you or your parents belong hand out financial aid, too.

- Loans and outright gifts come from Junior Achievement, Business and Professional Women, Jaycees, Boys' Clubs and Women's Clubs, to name a few.

- Career-minded groups finance studies in law enforcement, nursing and other health care fields. Check out all personal contacts you may have among the hundreds of such groups that sponsor students.

- Those of you who are active in church youth programs also have a natural aid. For example, Ann is a member of the United Methodist Church. Thus, she is eligible for a sizable loan. And were she planning to enter some form of Christian service, she would have even more financial aid assured her. Other faiths and denominations have similar student supports.

- Your alma mater may have endowed scholarships, too, that you will want to investigate. In most schools, you must apply for these. They are not prizes for the highest grades. You have to fill out a form that indicates your financial need, extracurricular and school activities and your college and career choices.

  At Norwin High School (Pennsylvania), for example, the John Rodgers $10,000 scholarship goes to one senior each year. Besides the above items, class rank is a factor. But most important is the final vote in your favor by the entire teaching faculty. No easy prize!

6. **You have it made if you excel in a sport, for sports scholarships have been around a long time.** Spotters for colleges and universities watch you play and try to recruit you.

- Mike, a 6'7" basketball player on the winning state team, showed his public speaking class 20 letters, wooing him to as many colleges all over the United States.

- Bill, another super-athlete, literally had everything provided except a washcloth when he went to Tulane University on a four-year basketball scholarship.

- And now over 500 colleges and universities are giving millions of dollars in athletic scholarships to women. You young women can count on handouts if you excel in swimming, soccer, volleyball or gymnastics.

7. **Lastly, write for special bulletins and reports.** Such a report is "Undergraduate Programs of Cooperative Education in the U.S. and Canada," which is free. Write to:

> National Commission for Cooperative
> Education
> 360 Huntington Ave.
> Boston, Massachusetts 02115

8. **In the meantime, hound your guidance people and librarians until you have read everything they have on financial aid for higher education.** Be the best-informed kid in school. And if you are smart enough, go to college for free!

STUDY PALMISTRY

How long will you live? Look at your palms — the palms of your hands, that is. You won't really find out. But you can have fun checking out this ancient source of foretelling the future. And if you know anything about palmistry, you are sure to be a party-upper.

If you have had your palm read, you know the major lines to be studied. They include:

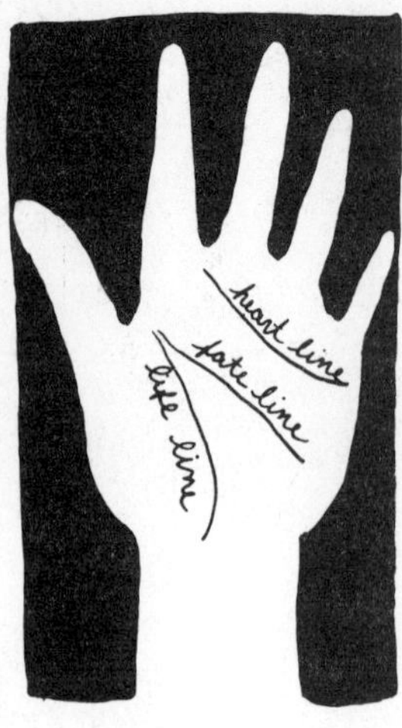

- your life line, which runs around the base of the thumb.

- your head line, which begins between the thumb and index finger and usually joins to the life line part of the way.

- your heart line, which crosses the hand.

- your fate line, which ideally begins at the rascette line and climbs to the Mount of Saturn.

Besides these major lines (with all their crosses, dots, stars and squares), all your hand characteristics are significant in reading your destiny. Palmistry takes these characteristics into account: the shape of your hand, its size, its hardness, its dryness and the thickness of your fingers.

Are you confused? Then pick up a library book on palmistry. Study the pictures. Compare your own hands with the drawings. Using a magnifying glass, look at the lines on your hand in good light, preferably sunlight. Note color, length, depth and number. Any of the pictural palmistry books have the same general interpretations. They rehash writings of early Greeks and later major practitioners. Some texts are easier to understand than others. All treat the subject seriously.

MORE WAYS TO LEARN MORE:

Debate **current issues.** Discuss **books, movies** and **television shows. Dream** — and learn to **interpret dreams.** Enroll in a **correspondence course. Interview pioneers** in your town. **Read a book. Read magazines** that are new to you. **Recruit experts** in your area to talk with you and your friends. **Speed-read.** (Take a mini-course, if necessary.) Study the **Bible.** Study the **stock market.** Talk to **people of other religions and ethnic groups.** Try **new foods.** Watch **educational television.**

Earn Dollars and Sense

GET A JOB

Do you want a job? Great. Before you start looking, though, here is advice from some of your peers. They're experienced — at least in looking for jobs.

- **Dylene:** "What bugged me when I was looking for a job was that they'd say, 'We'll call you.' Only they never did. I'd spend hours waiting for them to call, either to say I had the job or that they didn't want me. Finally, I learned that you have to follow up on applications. *You have to call them back* and let them know that you are really interested. That makes them interested in you and you get the job."

- **Allen:** "Plus, you can't settle for filling out one or two applications. *You have to get out there and cover the whole potential job market.* They aren't going to come looking for you, that's for sure."

- **Benson:** "Right — unless they know you or are a relative or something. *You have to work hard to get a job.* A lot of teen-agers put in an application and sit around waiting. As Dylene said, it doesn't work that way."

- **Brenda:** "Another thing that is important is *how you dress.* I've seen guys come into the Pizza Hut where I work, and they really look terrible. I guess they don't realize this is the first impression they are making on the person who does the hiring. Just looking at them, I know they won't get hired. Sure, they can do the work. They just don't have that clean-cut image most fast food places want. So how you dress is really important."

- **Tammy:** "Another thing to think about when you are looking for work is being on time. A lot of people seem to think that teen-agers are irresponsible. Whether or not that is a group fault of ours, many people *think* it is. So if you have a set time for an interview, *you'd better be there on time* or a little early. Then they'll know you are dependable.

ADVERTISE JOB WANTED, SERVICE OFFERED OR ITEM FOR SALE

At least one city newspaper runs free student want ads anually in June. Anyone in high school is eligible. Although that probably is not your local newspaper's policy — so you'll have to pay by the word — advertising your job or service wishes may mean money in your pockets.

A want ad doesn't guarantee a job, of course. Other variables influence responses to it, such as:

- how you word the ad
- who reads it
- whether it's timed to an opening

Also, it merely opens doors. You still have to be interviewed. You have to sell yourself.

Nonetheless, want ads get results. Therefore, to help you word your own, here are samples, screened from 500 student free ads. They hooked this reader because they are novel and/or honest.

- Intelligent young boy wants office job (sorting, packing, filing, stacking, lifting, errands, etc.). Friendly, polite, dependable worker.

- Will baby-sit in my home all day. Children 4-8. My mother is home all day with me.

- Loving care of your animals while you are on vacation.

- Reliable student will house-sit while you are away, light yard work and pets. References.

- Ex-candy striper, willing to help with elderly. Excellent references.

- Two young girls seek house, window, car, office cleaning.

- Restaurant job wanted: dishwasher, breader, pot-washer.

- Theater interest. On stage or backstage. Any job.

- Interested in dental hygienist work. Would appreciate training.

- Exercise your horse, groom, care for it. Experienced rider. Likes horses.

- Will clean and polish your golf clubs. $4 per set.

- Boats cleaned and waxed. No job too big.

- Have chain saw and lawn mower. Will cut and haul trees or mow your lawn. Very reasonable.

- Looking for clerical work. Have completed beginner's and advanced accounting and advanced mathematics courses, and have typing experience. Highly motivated.

Another money-maker is advertising salables — things you no longer use or need. Perhaps some of the items in those free ads will set you to brainstorming — or cleaning out your closet. They included:

- Armstrong student flute
- board games (have all pieces)
- train set
- used pony saddle in good condition
- Juliette stereo system
- Mickey Mouse record player
- parakeet
- canoe
- movie camera Yamaha 125 Enduro
- girl's bedroom set
- dirt bike
- mice for pets or snake food
- two-seater go-cart
- camping equipment, backpack
- hair dryer
- electric bass guitar
- Jean Littler junior golf set
- fishing rod
- scuba tanks
- aquarium

In buying want ads, don't forget your weekly neighborhood shopper. Often, those are read more than the city papers.

And while you are writing that ad, make 3" x 5" cards (typed or printed) to post on bulletin boards in laundromats, supermarkets, churches, community centers or condominium or apartment lobbies near you.

BABY-SIT FOR DOLLARS

Do you like children? Then baby-sitting is a lucrative way to spend your time — fellows as well as girls. If you don't like kids, forget it! You will be miserable, since they can try your patience. They will drive you up a wall, unless you appreciate their childishness and meet it head-on.

Whether you are a beginner or have had some experience, the following do's and don'ts will add to your effectiveness and the children's safety. At least, so say the teen-agers who compiled them.

1. **Know something about the parents and family.**
   Never go into a strange setting without checking beforehand. If a stranger calls you to baby-sit, ask who recommended you. Call that person and find out all you can about the family.

2. **Visit the home ahead of time.**
   Try to learn as many details as possible about the parents' preferences in child care. Learn where the baby paraphernalia, such as diapers, bottles, blankets, clothing and toys, is. What about formula-making, in case parents are gone longer than the present supply holds out? Ask questions about bedtime routine, snacks and what television shows the children are allowed to watch. Find out what their boundaries are in the house and yard. In other words, anticipate the questions for which you'll want answers when you are in charge later.

   Meet the children. While you are there with the parents, make sure the children understand your relationship to them: make sure they know that you will be in command when alone with them, and that they are to obey you. Try to win their approval of you by being friendly, sincere and interested in them.

   Learn the complete house plan during this initial visit. Where is the master switch box, in case the lights go off? How do the doors lock and unlock? Where are the light switches in the rooms you will be using? Where is first aid equipment kept?

Ask that parents leave emergency lists beside the telephone. First, look for a permanent one with numbers of the doctor, police, fire department, ambulance service and neighbors who can be called in a hurry. A second sheet should have the name, address and telephone number of the place where parents can be reached on the particular day or night you are sitting.

Also, while talking with the parents this first time, clarify your exact responsibilities. Will your duties include preparing meals? bathing the children? taking telephone messages? How many hours (approximately) will you be expected to be in charge?

And because this is a business for you, ask what the parents plan to pay you for your services. If you feel the offer is not enough, say so now. Don't wait until after you have baby-sat — and then complain. If asked to set your own fee, charge according to number of children and their ages, the amount of work expected from you, your own experience and the going rate among your baby-sitting peers.

3. **On the day or night you baby-sit, make your responsibility a full-time job.** Keep your eyes on the child (or children) *all the time.* Kids move fast. A 3-year-old could climb up drawers to top shelves in the kitchen cupboards where medicines are supposedly out of her reach. A toddler might flush toys down the toilet, to the tune of a big plumbing bill.

The child's safety is your number one priority. Therefore, beware of strangers at the door, and let no one in whom you can't identify. If you think you have prowlers or window-peekers, call the police immediately. In case of fire, grab the baby and shoo the older children out of the house. Herd them to safety away from the house. *Then* call the fire department.

What about the actual sitting — that time after the children are asleep? Don't go to sleep yourself, or get so engrossed in a television show that you forget your responsibilities. Check on the baby frequently. You want no crib deaths. Check on toddlers, too. They get uncovered or fall out of bed or wander around, long after you think they are asleep. Sometimes they play tricks on you, too, like hiding under the bed or in their toy closet, and falling asleep there.

Assume no refrigerator privileges, except those the parents have offered you. And even then, don't eat them out of the next day's dinner. Don't snoop. After all, you are a guest, even though a hired one. Nor should your friends telephone you, or you phone them. Keep the lines free. And definitely do not entertain your friends at the house where you are sitting. They are distractions from your line of duty.

One last caution: keep in touch with home base. Your parents should have your telephone number. And don't think you have failed your job if you call your mother or dad when emergencies arise. One girl, whose mother is a nurse, frantically phoned her when an 8-year-old nearly cut off her toe with a garden shovel. The sitter was only half a block away from home and had immediate help.

Again, call your parents to come and get you if the person who had planned to drive you home is drunk. Your safety should also be part of the baby-sitting contract.

Your responsibility as a baby-sitter is big. That's why you should be paid well. That's also why you should never relax your vigil while on the job.

CREATE YOUR OWN BUSINESS OR SERVICE

Jump the gun! Beat your peers to job openings by being your own boss. Look around you. What service is needed? What new job can you create?

Then make a preliminary survey to determine its monetary or service value to you and to the community. Question neighbors and people who would be affected or involved. Will it take initial capital? How much time would you devote to it? How many other teen-agers in your area are doing the same thing — or are you originating the idea? Is there really a need for this job or service? If your original idea doesn't pass this preliminary investigation, think up another. Check out its possibilities the same way. When one does click, get started before another teen-ager beats you to it.

Activities you can capitalize on are varied. Several were listed pre-viously, under advertising. Other ideas are:

- making and selling homemade bread
- growing and selling herbs
- raising and selling worms

- making and selling crafts: pot-holders, hooked rugs, T-shirts with lettering and designs, leather purses and belts, minia-ture patchwork items, jewelry (copper or shell) or ceramics

- chauffeuring for someone who can no longer drive

- operating a home candy kitchen

- publishing a neighborhood news sheet

- refinishing furniture

- hiring out to take charge of birthday parties

- training dogs

- traveling as a companion with an older person

- being a live-in baby-sitter for a family, accompanying them on their vacation

- taking pictures of your friends and developing and enlarging the photos. One teen-ager apprenticed with a photographer long enough to learn the basics. Now he has set up his own business. He takes wedding pictures.

- mending and altering clothes, if you like to sew

- being on call to run errands, shop or taxi

- offering a typing service (if you are qualified). Do résumés, manuscripts and business letters.

Whatever you do, the old saw still holds: you must build a *better* mousetrap. Quality counts!

CREATE YOUR OWN BUSINESS:
BUY AND SELL FLOWERS DOOR-TO-DOOR

Start your own flower business by serving two needs. Buy your flowers from retired people who have their own flower gardens, overflowing with a profusion of blossoms. And sell to high-rise apartment-dwellers who have no home-grown flowers at all.

1. **Contact all possible flower sources.**
   You will want to make your own financial arrangements, of course. But here are alternative suggestions you may want to consider:

   - If the gardeners have more flowers than they can physically care for, offer to help with gardening chores in return for flowers you can sell.

   - Purchase the blossoms outright, setting your wholesale price high enough to make the retiree gardeners happy, and low enough for you to profit.

   - Split sales income 50-50.

2. **Prepare sample nosegays to woo future customers.**

3. **Deliver these to anyone you know in high-rise apartments.** (You will need contacts within these carefully controlled units.) Explain your sales venture. Ask if the party would be interested in a $2 , $3 or $5 bouquet, to be delivered at the same time once a week.

4. **Widen possible sales contacts.**
   From known clients, try to get names of people they recommend. The newspaper carrier for a given apartment complex is another source for names. Take names from the directory (or intercom buzzers) in apartment entrances and telephone each prospect. (Although most multiple housing units allow no solicitors on the premises, telephone contacts are still legal.)

Your success in carrying through this enterprise will depend on *you.* How businesslike are you in selling, collecting and keeping accounts straight? If you are efficient, profits are here — both for you and for your co-sponsors.

CREATE YOUR OWN BUSINESS: CLEAN CARPETS

Tim needed money desperately. How could he get some fast — like today — he wondered. Then the idea hit him.

"Mom, if I clean our living room carpet, will you pay for the steamer and cleaning fluid?"

"That's a deal," his mother said. "When do you start?"

"Right now."

Tim rented the equipment at the corner drug store. He cleaned the off-white carpet thoroughly. His mother was pleased — especially since Tim had initiated the idea. So when he asked if he might have the remainder of the rug shampoo, she agreed. "For your room?" she asked.

But Tim had other ideas. The equipment was rented for a 24-hour period. No discount if returned early. Thus he had free use of it, once the family rug-cleaning was finished.

Tim went to his next-door neighbor, soliciting business. "Yes," said Mrs. Brownell, "you may clean the halls. We won't have to move furniture, and the carpet is badly soiled. How much do you charge?"

They agreed on $15. Tim did the job in half an hour, bought another bottle of rug shampoo with part of his profits, and visited another neighbor. By dusk, he had cleaned five entryways. He grossed $75.

That was the start of a part-time business with rented equipment. Because he lived in a garden condominium, he had it made. All units were carpeted with light colors that needed frequent cleaning, at least in the high-traffic areas.

Perhaps you can follow suit.

CREATE YOUR OWN BUSINESS: MAKE CORSAGES

With the price of corsages constantly rising, what competition you can give the florists! Take orders from your school friends at prom time, for instance. Make your own corsages at a third of the commercial price. Make money for yourself or your favorite charity. It has been done.

Lillian Glover pins her homemade corsages on delegates at state conventions of the Illinois Parent-Teacher Association. She charges $2 for the larger ones, and $1 for the smaller clusters and boutonnieres.

Through this activity, she has raised $100,000 to send kids to college. Admittedly, her sales cover more years than you are old, but never once has she raised her price. Therefore, if she can make a profit at those give-away figures, why can't you make money in a corsage business?

1. **First, find a flower source.**
    Contact individuals you know who raise roses, gardenias, baby's breath and violets in their own gardens. Check with wholesalers as to their prices and the quantity you must buy to deal with them. Scan open fields for possible sources of daisies and black-eyed Susans that are yours for the picking.

2. **Make up a few samples.**
    Wear one to school or church. When anyone asks about it, explain your intent to make them for sale. Give a few to friends to wear for a special date or occasion, to whip up interest in your project.

3. **Advertise.**
    Use a small ad in your school paper, shopper's weekly or church letter. Place bright floral-decorated signs on free bulletin boards. Talk up your business.

4. **Plan ahead for special days.**
    Besides the proms, look to other school events, like graduation or homecoming. Also, aim for calendar events that florists feature, such as Christmas, Valentine's Day, Easter, Mother's Day and Grandparent's Day.

5. **Take orders far enough ahead of time so you can fill them on time.**

6. **Be sure you have space, refrigeration if necessary, ribbons, wire and corsage pins.**

7. **Take on only those orders you can personally handle,** unless you plan to pay helpers.

8. **Keep records.**
    When a customer is satisfied, you can repeat the same arrangement because you have recorded it. Costs and profits must be carefully listed. Remember, this is a business, and no matter how big or small, bookkeeping is as important as product.

CREATE YOUR OWN BUSINESS: MAKE AND RENT COSTUMES

You don't have to sew fancy creations to make costumes. All you need are staples, pins, iron-on tape, needle and thread for a few basic stitches and recycled clothes to alter.

In fact, you could have a thriving business by conjuring up children's Halloween costumes. Kids want something different each year. Stores charge outrageous prices for bits of cheap cambric, boxed as ghost or pirate costumes. And you can make better costumes for next to nothing.

1. **First, you need ideas, such as:** hobo, bride, tooth fairy, tightrope-walker, Spanish dancer, guru, clown, Pilgrim, nurse, cowboy, Disneyland characters.

2. **Next, you need old clothes.**
Before you throw away anything, check for possible costume use. Old leotards are basics for Elizabethan, pirate and animal costumes. An old cape makes a Superman. Black lace blouses become Spanish mantillas. Even a moth-eaten jacket and frayed, patched pants suit a hobo.

3. **For pirate, gypsy and royalty creations, check your family's old costume jewelry:** beads, baubles, bracelets, pendants and even single earrings.

4. **Solicit your neighbors for their cast-offs, too.**
Perhaps you will become heir to a gold mine, such as one lady gave to her neighbor's children to use in playing dress-up:

   - taffeta formal dresses
   - a Prince Albert coat
   - a man's complete formal attire
   - a velvet 1890s dress

5. **Also, visit thrift shops, rummage sales and Goodwill stores.** Often, you can pick up outdated dresses and suits that are terrific costumes, just as they are. Air what you purchase, and pack with sachet.

6. **With a little imagination and a dash of dexterity, you can fashion symbols that lend authenticity to costumes.** Conjure up space helmets out of cardboard, paper clips and silver paint. Staple red construction paper hearts all over a white formal for a Queen of Hearts costume. Stuff leotard or pantyhose legs and sew them on either side of the middle of a bodysuit for a spider.

7. **Box costumes as you assemble them.**
Place in separate containers. Label each with the kind of costume and the appropriate child's size and age.

8. **Now advertise throughout your neighborhood and school.**

Your best timing is just before Halloween. Once you are known, however, you can expect all sorts of strange requests throughout the year for special events, such as theme parties (Gay Nineties, King Neptune, historical character masquerade), plays, pageants and parades. Costume rental stores are few. Hence, you may have little or no competition, which is in your favor.

CREATE YOUR OWN BUSINESS: OPERATE AN ANTIQUE PHOTO STUDIO

All you need is a Polaroid camera and a closet full of old-fashioned clothes (bought, begged or borrowed). No doubt you have seen one of the 50 antique photo studios doing a thriving business throughout the United States. Disney World has one, for example, on Main Street.

1. **Ape their techniques and paraphernalia.**

2. **Take pictures of your friends — singles, couples or whole families — costumed in Gay Nineties apparel.**

3. **Mount the finished instant photo in an antique-style frame.** Often, you can find old photographs, mounted on heavy cardboard, taken in the late 1800s or early 1900s. Rip off the old picture. Glue on the one you just took. For a dime or two spent at Goodwill or a garage sale, you have a frame as old as the clothes.

5. **The professional antique photographers sell for $8 what costs them 40 cents.** You aren't professional yet, so charge according to results you get in your picture-taking. Increase your profits as you gain professionalism.

6. **Offer your services at church and charity events.** Give profits to those causes. Publicize your activity this way.

CREATE YOUR OWN BUSINESS: ORGANIZE A TEEN-AGE JOB AGENCY

Have you thought of starting a youth job agency? If you are ambitious, outgoing, dependable, self-disciplined and enjoy a people-challenge, this is for you. Not only can such an agency be lucrative; it will also serve both teen-agers and the community at large.

Look around you. Survey possibilities for jobs.

- Take that vacant lot at the corner, for instance. Owned by an out-of-towner, it has been a weed patch for years. Recently, someone has dumped rubbish there. Write the owner; describe the mess; offer to clean it up and keep the lot in shape for a price. Perhaps you will get a permanent assignment.

- The elderly couple who live in that old Victorian mansion have allowed their property to deteriorate, too, because of poor health and inadequate help. You could take on that assignment, were you to have enough teen-aged employees.

- Those summer people on the lake a few miles out of town — they used to have a permanent caretaker. But live-in help is hard to find. Hence, where they once had a prize garden, now weeds choke the perennials. The owners have money. They would welcome youth helping on a summer assignment, or even doing year-round caretaking.

Your community has similar opportunities, plus window-cleaning, minor repairing, putting up screens and storm windows, trimming hedges, escorting the elderly to clinics, chauffeuring a widow who does not drive, shopping for shut-ins and sitting with a bedridden invalid. And, of course, there is always housework. Look around you. Probe. Determine needs. If the prospects are challenging enough, talk to those acquaintances of yours who are looking for something to do. Get their commitment to take jobs you line up for them. With teen-age backing, you can start your project.

1. **First, have the would-be employees sign up as they would in any employment agency, giving vital statistics, type of work wanted and pay scale desired.** Keep these applications on file. Match them with job requests that come to you.

2. **Advertise, using an attention-getting name,** such as "Teen-aged Job-Tacklers." (Or is that too corny?) Advertise on every free bulletin board in town, at supermarkets, community centers, laundromats, churches and at the American Association of Retired Persons.

    Make attractive "situations wanted" posters for this purpose. Change posters often enough to keep them fresh and vital. Even change size, color and wording. Mimeograph handbills to pass out to neighbors. Telephone. Write letters. Contact local service clubs. Tell everyone you know, and the story will grow. Put small ads in free newspapers.

3. **Take requests by telephone.**
    Unless you know the person calling, ask for a reference. Check out this party and place *before* you send your workers to the job. You can't be too careful. One casualty would ruin your business. Send your workers out in teams of two or three, depending on the job.

4. **You can collect fees two ways.**
    Ask teen-agers for 10 percent of their first paycheck on each job assignment. Or ask employers to send you a perquisite on completion of a satisfactory job. This way, you are off the hook for service complaints.

5. **Continually check up.**
    Visit teen-agers on their jobs. Inspect work done. Directly inquire of employers.

    For example, a boy called his own employer and asked, "Would you like to have your lawn mowed?" And when the man said that he already had a boy doing the job, the youngster asked,

"But are you satisfied with his work?"

"Definitely!" replied the employer.

You can check up as subtly.

The potential is tremendous, once you start your own youth employment agency. You can even turn it into a career, with the right breaks. But move cautiously. Ask a lawyer friend about possible legal involvements. Talk with someone who knows the agency business, like a person in the state employment bureau.

With your eyes open, you can be a future community leader by serving now.

CREATE YOUR OWN BUSINESS: REFINISH FURNITURE

The antique craze has made furniture-stripping a profitable part-time business. Todd is so intrigued by his enterprise that he's been known to skip school to finish an order.

"Not that I recommend playing hooky. It's just that I get so involved that I lose all sense of time," Todd explained to some classmates. "But if I didn't get 'high' from seeing the smooth satiny finish after hours and hours of scraping and finishing, I'd admit it is stinking, tedious work."

1. **Apprentice under someone like Todd who knows what it's all about.**

2. **Or buy a stripping kit in a hardware store or a store's home furnishing department.** Directions are included. Read them. Start with an old piece of your own. Experiment.

3. **If you like making old look new and scraping paint off to reveal beautiful natural woods, then practice until you feel confident you know the technique.**

4.   **Now you are ready to renovate other people's cherished antiques.**

CREATE YOUR OWN BUSINESS: SELL BALLOONS

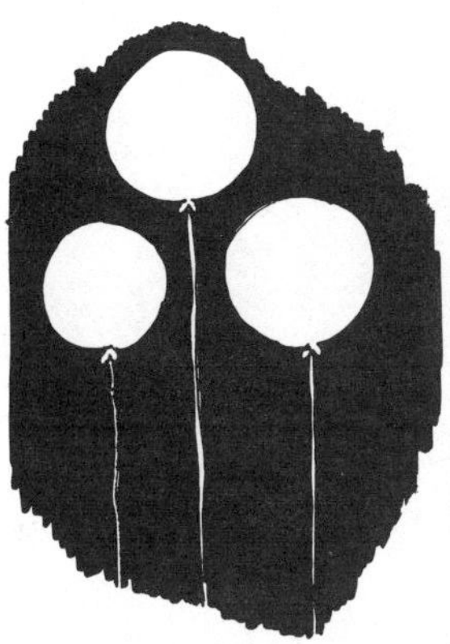

In place of flowers, offer a 21-balloon salute. This is a new way to remember a birthday, anniversary, holiday, graduation or winning event.

1.   **Offer to send a salute (for a price, of course) to anyone within delivery range of your home.**

2.   **Fill with helium 21 different-colored balloons.** Arrange on various lengths of string, floating upward from a painted flower pot.

3.   **Deliver as you would a floral gift.**

Here's a quick money-maker if you're selling balloons individually:

4.   **Bid to sell balloons at any local street fairs, fire-fighters' or policemen's carnivals, county fairs or church bazaars.**

5.   **Buy balloons wholesale and sell them (full of helium) for a good deal more.** Kids can't resist them. You don't even have to call out your wares. The balloons, floating around the seller's head, advertise themselves.

6.   **You can either pocket your profits or sell for your youth group at church functions.** When it is your personal business, you will be assessed a percentage or entrance fee. If proceeds you earn go for church or charities, your concession will be gratis, no doubt.

START A SECOND-TIME-AROUND BUSINESS

Second-hand stuff makes money. Scan flea markets, thrift shops and rummage sales, and see for yourself. Then set up your own business.

1. **Start with a child's wagon-load of old costume jewelry, records, books and outgrown clothes that you have salvaged from family discards.** Pay the small fee to set yourself up in a local flea market. Give the project an honest try two or three times.

2. **Otherwise, set up your garage with the same merchandise.** Advertise your sale by placing a placard or banner on your parked car in front of the garage. Place signs and arrows at the main corners, pointing the way.

3. **For a bigger business, find yourself a storage area.** A room, out-building, barn — any space that can hold rummage until you sell — gives you the edge over other garage sales.

   For some reason, only merchandisers of second-hand items are ready with cash to buy used furnishings. For next to nothing, they clear out what a tenant doesn't want to move. Be on the spot at the right time, and you will get a tape recorder, type-writer, lamp and desk — or the like — as Rick did when his neighbor moved to Florida.

4. **You will need transportation for these pick-ups.** Borrow a truck or small trailer for those special times when you can have furniture free. Otherwise, the family automobile will suffice for hand-carried stuff — dishes, clothes, utensils, picture frames, etc.

5. **Advertise.** If people who are moving know your phone number, they will gladly call you, rather than lug stuff to charity boxes or leave it in the trash. They want immediate clearance, though. What you pick up is 100 percent profit to you, and a service for the

party calling you. Post your pick-up and sale notices wherever the law allows. Put placards in laundromats, vacant store windows and on supermarkets' bulletin boards. Put mimeographed flyers on the windshields of parked cars. Pay for an ad in local newspaper want-ad sections.

6. **Make a business out of your sales, as long as you have enough merchandise.** Keep a sales schedule. Perhaps it can be a monthly one. Inventory stored goods periodically, to make sure you bring out seasonal items in season.

    Occasionally, try gimmicks for sales, such as:

    - a silent auction
    - a give-away table
    - door prizes

    Also, when selling, don't price items too high. People go to garage sales and flea markets for bargains, and as long as you have the items on hand, you don't have the cash. By organizing your pick-up and sales activities systematically, you can keep profitably busy throughout your teens.

ENTER CONTESTS

Win $10,000! Merla Sue did! True, everyone who enters a contest doesn't win. On the other hand, you can't win unless you *do* enter.

Take the Voice of Democracy contest, annually open to all senior high-school students throughout the United States. Merla Sue Hansell, a senior at Troy High School in Illinois at the time, wrote and taped a 650-word oration on "Why I Care About America." She won the local school contest, and those at the county, state and national levels. Not counting any of the previous wins, the national prize was $10,000 in college scholarships. That's $50 a word, a neat pay-off for entering the contest.

Nor was she the only winner. The Voice of Democracy contest pays cash gifts and scholarships to thousands of teen-agers like yourself. Sponsored by the Veterans of Foreign Wars and Auxiliary, this three- to five-minute taped script contest is repeated every fall. And someone wins in each local contest.

Bob Koncerak, for instance, won a $300 first prize at Norwin Senior High School in Irwin, Pennsylvania. He added another $100 to his winnings by placing third in the county contest.

Many similar national contests are open to teen-agers. The American Legion has an annual oratorical contest dealing with the Constitution. The *Atlantic Monthly* sponsors a short story contest.

On local levels, contests are posted from time to time. Although they aren't tagged with as big prizes as those in national contests, they are lucrative and give you a sense of accomplishment. Enter "Help the Handicapped" poster contests. Watch for environmental slogan contests. Try writing advertising gimmicks.

- For example, Donna Ray won $25 for 50 words about "Mother." Her English teacher announced the contest, sponsored by a neighborhood mall. Donna wrote her paragraph in 15 minutes, submitted it the next day, and received the prize three days later.

- Jason heard a limmerick contest announced on TV. All winning submissions would be used to advertise a new real estate project. Jason wrote three and mailed them on his way to school the next morning. Two weeks later, he received a telephone call: "Two of your limericks have won prizes. Fifty dollars is in the mail for you."

And you may get excited over mail-order prizes, like those available through contests sponsored by Publisher's Clearing House, *Reader's Digest* and catalogs. Your chances of winning aren't too great. But just entering and watching for announcements of the winners can keep the adrenalin flowing. There's always that chance of winning *if* you enter.

GET A PAPER ROUTE

Delivering newspapers is an excellent way to ease into the world of business. You learn to be dependable, to be on time, to take your work seriously, to keep accurate records and to get along with people — all kinds. You are getting work experience.

Later, you can use this on job applications and résumés as previous experience. Having been a newspaper carrier holds prestige with many employers.

Sometimes, the job can grow as you grow.

For example, Dave, now 18, has a paper route of 750 customers. "I manage to roll the paper, put a rubber band around it, and throw it fairly accurately on the doorstep while I'm driving the car," he says. "The police know me. Otherwise they would probably think I was loony, I guess. I manage to cover the round in an hour and a half."

Dave started peddling papers on a short route when he was 12. Each year he has added to it, and now he boasts about the biggest route in his city. He has even worked out a coupon book for patrons to pay three months in advance — and save him those weekly door-to-door collections.

HOLD A SILENT AUCTION

Is your class raising money for that cruise you are planning? Will your scout troop be able to get funds for a summer camping trip in Europe? Does your youth group need more cash to meet its church pledge? If so, try a silent auction.

This is one of the easiest fund-raisers. Have each member provide an item (or two or three) to be auctioned. Place these things around the room, allowing each its share of viewing space. Give every member and guest present small cards. Explain that if a person wishes to bid on a particular item, he or she is to write an amount and his or her name on one of these cards. The bidder places it under the item, or alongside it, face-down. No peeking at another's bid card is allowed.

After everyone has made the rounds and bid, the committee takes over. One member picks up the cards under or near the first item, checks the bids and announces the highest bid. The winner pays for the article *before* the next piece is awarded the same way.

Auctioned items need not be new, as long as they have bidding appeal. Homemade items usually bring high bids. Try:

- candy
- baked goods
- ceramics
- craft items of all kinds
- records and tapes
- jewelry — slightly used
- books, magazines and comic books
- stamps (packaged for amateur collectors)
- paintings and plaques
- stuffed animals
- individual pieces of clothing if new or worn once, maybe. (You don't want rummage.)

Since an auctioneer doesn't whip up that sense of competition, you never make as much from a silent auction as you would from a fast-paced regular one. However, what you make is pure profit. Very little planning is required. Everything goes for some cash, since even one bid on an article sells it. And it can be either a social event or one attached to a regular meeting of your organization.

HOUSE-SIT

The public is scared. Vandals and thieves have forced whole neighborhoods to employ 24-hour security patrols. Burglar alarm companies are making millions.

You, too, can cash in on a service that deters break-ins. Offer to house-sit when neighbors are away.

Such a business requires the following:

- appreciation that you are being trusted with valuable property
- trustworthiness
- reliability in following through with responsibilities
- dedication to details

Once you have a house to care for, get the following information *before* the residents leave:

- How do things such as the sprinkler, locks, shutters and light switches work?

- Where is the main fuse box?

- Is basement-flooding a possibility?

- Where is the smoke alarm?

Insist on a list of emergency numbers for you to call. You'll want the phone numbers of the police and fire department, the plumber, air-conditioner and furnace services and a number where you can reach the owners, if possible.

Put down in black and white exactly what the owners expect you to do, and get their signatures on the agreement.

They may ask you to:

- rotate lights

- walk through all rooms during a daily visit

- let in the exterminator (if you are in the South)

- water plants

- feed goldfish

- check all locks

- water the lawn (if there is no gardener)

- pick up all papers, flyers or items left on doorsteps — anything

that indicates an empty house.

- any other responsibilities you and the tenant agree you will assume

Personally make contact with the police, as soon as you have the job. Indicate the number of days you will be in charge. Let them know your expected pattern — when you will be visiting the premises. If they also assume neighborhood cruising and checking when residents are on vacation, try to fit your schedule with theirs — arriving at different times so as to prolong the security.

Charge your clients according to time spent on the job. Or have a set fee. Give an estimate in advance. Bill and collect like any operating business.

JOIN A CULINARY CREW

Teen-agers who participated were excited about this international event. They served important people from all over the world, and talked about them for weeks afterwards.

Volkswagen had opened its New Stanton, Pennsylvania, plant with a gourmet luncheon. To serve it, they recruited home economics students from neighboring high schools. "The pay was terrific. The experience was out of this world," according to one of the fellows who served.

This is an example of chance encounters culinary crews have to serve public and private parties. Other corporations, churches and service clubs call for help from time to time. That's why a well-organized food-serving crew has a place in any community.

1. **Yours can be either a service or paid crew — or both.** Either way, you usually get fed very well. You have fun while helping others. And when you are paid, you are paid well.

2. **To serve effectively, you may want to follow this**

pattern, worked out by one church youth group:

- First, those interested in serving asked a home economics teacher to give them pointers in acceptable grooming, courtesies and food-serving techniques.

- Next, one of the older youths took charge. She became the liaison between crew and dinner groups. She set up schedules, determined number of servers needed, and contacted the teen-agers on call.

- At the time of the dinner, this particular crew worked in teams of six. They came to and went from tables in this formation:

    - The first person approached the table empty-handed and lifted the fruit cups from the first two places.

    - The second waiter set down the dinner plates of food in front of those first two guests and picked up the fruit cups from the third and fourth places.

    - The third crew member put down the dinner plates at the empty spaces and picked up the next two fruit cups.

    - This routine continued for all six servers, covering 12 places.

    - With fast service from the kitchen, often the first server was back, ready to put down the plates in places 11 and 12, left empty by the sixth server.

    - They followed the same routine for dessert.

    - The technique became almost flawless, with time between serving the main course and dessert for pouring coffee.

The system is worth copying if you are serious about organizing a culinary crew.

MORE MONEY-MAKING IDEAS:

Be a **pet-sitter. Chauffeur** for someone who has an automobile but can no longer drive. **Train dogs. Walk dogs. Travel as a companion** with an older person. **Exercise horses. Wash windows** (ask to be paid per pane). **Give music lessons** to beginners (if you are proficient). **Raise** and **sell worms. Make deliveries** (on call). **Wax cars. Wrap** and **mail packages.** Care for **plants or gardens. Raise plants** from cuttings. **Tailor** and **make alterations.**

ABOUT THE AUTHOR

Shirley Pollock has worked with teen-agers most of her adult life. She has taught communication courses in Pennsylvania high schools and at Western Michigan University. She has judged national debate tournaments, been parliamentarian at student congresses, conducted Voice of Democracy contests and guided school newspaper staffs.

In the churches her husband, the Reverand James R. Pollock, served in Connecticut, Michigan, Wisconsin and Pennsylvania, Mrs. Pollock worked with teens and college students. She also directed church camps and counseled on church college campuses. Four daughters kept the parsonage bustling with teens and young adults, too. She and her family have traveled together around the world, visiting and camping throughout Europe, South America, Africa, China, India, Japan and many countries in between.

All of this youth involvement punctuates Shirley Pollock's freelance writing. She writes *for* teens in *Seventeen, Scholastic, Coed* and *4HTeen.* She writes *about* teens for parents, youth leaders and counselors. Some 60 periodicals have published her articles. Among them are *Parents, Today's Education, Christian Home, Family Life Today, Home Life* and *Guideposts.*

Her two previously published books are *Youth Worker's Success Manual* (Abingdon) and *Adventures in Being a Parent* (Standard Publishing).

Other books by Shirley Pollock:

- ***Adventures in Being a Parent (Standard Publishing)***
- ***Youth Worker's Success Manual (Abingdon)***